HOW TO PICK UP GIRLS!

Discover exactly how to meet beautiful women. In bars, buses, trains — even on the street!

The fool proof guide to meeting women without a formal introduction.

**by
Eric Weber**

**SYMPHONY PRESS
TENAFLY, NEW JERSEY**

Printing History:

1st Printing .... December 1970
2nd Printing ....March 1971
3rd Printing .... August 1971
4th Printing .... December 1971
5th Printing ....March 1972
6th Printing ....September 1972
7th Printing .... January 1973
8th Printing ....May 1973
9th Printing .... October 1973
10th Printing...................................... January 1974
11th Printing.....................................September 1974
12th Printing..July 1975
13th Printing..................................... November 1975
14th Printing.. April 1976
15th Printing.....................................February 1977
16th Printing..................................... December 1977
17th Printing.....................................February 1979
18th Printing..May 1979
19th Printing..................................... December 1979
20th Printing.. April 1980
21st Printing .... July 1980 Revised Edition

ISBN 0-914094-00-9

*Dedicated to the
twenty-five beautiful girls
who helped so much
to write this book.*

TABLE OF CONTENTS

INTRODUCTION

Has this little tragedy ever happened to you?

You're walking down the street. Minding your own business. Wondering how the hell you're going to meet the next payment on your car. And suddenly you spot a girl.

Not just an ordinary girl. Not just a fantastic girl. But *the girl* — someone so absolutely sexy, so downright delicious-looking, you actually find yourself *running* to catch up with her

You've just got to see more of her long shapely legs. Her fine breasts. Her high, firm behind. For an instant you even consider grabbing her right there in the street.

As you close in on her your heart starts to pound like a kettle drum. You rack your brain. What can I say that will make her melt into a little pool of butter at my feet? How can I manage to hold her and bite her and hug her and plant kisses *all* over her wonderful, supple body?

Should I throw myself at her feet and promise her my savings account, my car—even my brand new stereo? Or should I just grab her long golden locks and drag her off into the sunset?

Your mind draws a blank. You don't know what to do. You worry, maybe she'll think my ears are too big. Maybe, God forbid, she'll notice my bald spot. You're terrified that if you do get up enough nerve to say something it'll be silly. She'll ignore you. Or even worse, she'll tell you to get lost. Or report you to the nearest cop. Or both!

So when you finally do catch up with her you don't say anything at all. You merely watch as she turns the corner and sashays out of your life forever.

And with a sudden rush of anguish you realize *never* will you slap her affectionately on the behind. Never will you nibble on her ear. Never will you get your eager little hands on her large soft breasts.

In the days and weeks to come you think of her. Often. More than you care to. And it drives you nuts. Why didn't you make contact with her? Why were you such a coward? If only there were something you could have said that would have made her take notice of you. Some magic little technique that would have gotten her to come with you. Talk with you. Kiss you and love you and everything with you.

Well, the fact is there's more than one little magic technique for picking up girls. There are literally thousands of them. And you'll find just about every one cf them right here in this book.

So happy reading. And then happier hunting!

THE REDHEAD THAT
GOT AWAY

Let's face it — most guys know how to handle a girl once they've been introduced to her. When you're visiting Aunt Hortense (the family matchmaker) and the cute, busty girl from next door just *happens* to drop by, that's a natural. It's all been set up for you.

The real problem is, how do you get introduced when there's no one around to introduce you? When the girl of your dreams happens to be a total stranger with an icy, bitchy glare in her eye? What do you say to her? How do you make contact without scaring her off?

Let me tell you how I went about solving this problem. I hate to admit it, but I happen to be a spectacularly ordinary guy. I'm not rich or good-looking. And the only woman who thinks I'm terribly charming is my mother.

Being ordinary, though, hasn't kept me from falling passionately in love with *extraordinary* women. I'm crazy about them. And all my life I've wondered if there weren't some great way of meeting the millions of luscious women I kept on seeing in restaurants, elevators, museums, etc.

The breaking point came about a year ago. I was riding on a bus. Across the aisle sat a beautiful redhead with huge, bright green eyes and large, heart-shaped lips that were begging to be kissed.

I stared at the redhead. She looked back at me. We both looked away. Then she looked at me. I looked at her. And we both looked away.

It was sort of like touching without using hands. I wanted to use hands. But before I could do that I knew I had to say something. I knew it was up to me to act.

But I couldn't. I was afraid. I didn't know what to say. And before I knew it, the bus stopped, the girl got off, and that was the last I ever saw of her.

I was crushed. For a brief moment I had flirted with a goddess. And then I'd blown it ... let it slip through my nervous little fingers. I was furious with myself. I vowed never would I let anything like that happen again.

But how could I do anything about it? How could I get over my paralysing fear?

Suddenly I had an *inspiration* . Why not ask real, live girls *exactly* what it would take to pick them up? Why not get the lowdown straight from the horse's mouth?

And that's just what I did. I interviewed twenty-five of the prettiest, hippest girls I knew. And asked them how I could go about meeting them if I'd never seen them in my life before. In other words, how could I pick them up?

This book is built around their answers. Answers which I think you'll find absolutely fascinating. For what these twenty-five girls had to say *really works*.

They told me real, tangible things to say and do that have actually helped me pick up girls. In fact, I've gotten to be real good at it.

And believe me, if a guy as ordinary as me can learn to pick up girls, *you* can become an expert.

THE FABULOUS TWENTY-FIVE

Before they tell you how to pick them up, you might like to know a little bit about the twenty-five girls I interviewed for this book.

First of all, they're single. Each and every one of them.

Second, they're terrific-looking. If you saw them all together in a group picture you'd think you were looking at a photo of a beauty contest. There are eight blondes, three redheads, and fourteen dazzling brunettes. I figured I might as well start with the girls I'd most like to pick up.

But, then, these girls have a lot more than looks going for them. One is a computer programmer, two are artists, two are teachers, three stewardesses, two executive secretaries, two models, one a singer, another an actress, and so on. They're all smart, poised, witty, and good talkers — the kind of girls you'd give at least one of your eye teeth to pick up.

And who knows, maybe after you've read and digested all their great advice here in this book, you'll see one of The Fabulous 25 sitting on a bus. Or in a restaurant. Or walking down the street. And instead of letting her get away as you might have done in the past, you'll put into action the very things she told you right here in this book. And you'll pick her up.

And won't that be terrific!

THE FIRST STEP

The first, and really the only thing it takes to pick up girls, is to talk to them. Basically, that's it. You find a girl who turns you on, you stroll right up to her, and you say, "That dimple on your left knee is absolutely sensational!" Or, "Why are you staring at me?" Or, "What's your name?"

Or you say any damn thing that pops into your head. That's all there is to it. If you can do that, you can really pick up girls. By the truckloads!

Unfortunately, there's a catch. Despite the fact it's easy as pie to pick up girls, most guys are afraid to try. Afraid they'll get rebuffed. It's really very sad. Millions of women are out there dying to get picked up. Yet the guys who are dying to pick them up are too scared to give them a tumble.

Fear, of course, is normal. But it's also very defeating. It can *paralyse* a man, keep him from even contemplating picking up a girl. And, brother, if you're afraid to *think* about picking up girls, you're sure as hell not going to pick any up.

That's why the first part of this book deals with overcoming fear and building up confidence. It's *incredibly* important!

And as you'll discover in the next few pages, no matter who you are or what you look like, you have every reason in the world to be supremely confident.

WHO GETS PICKED UP?

It's a good question. If you ask it of the average guy, you'll probably get an answer like this: "Picked up? Ugh! That's disgusting. My sister would never get picked up. Only fat girls in cheap perfume and red high heels get picked up. *Ugh!*"

And in a way, the average guy would be kind of right. Those kinds of women *do* get picked up.

But they're not the only ones. Not by a long shot. All sorts of women get picked up. Everywhere. Everyday. In every way.

Heiresses from Darien, Connecticut get picked up. So do secretaries from the Bronx. Skiers in Aspen, Colorado and schoolteachers in Kenosha, Wisconsin. Nice girls and smart girls and pretty girls and rich girls and show-girls and college girls and librarians — they all get picked up. A lot!

They might not call it getting picked up. A girl might say, "I *met* the nicest guy on the bus yesterday," or, "I *chatted* with a very rich-looking man on the elevator this morning." But what she's really saying is, "I got picked up." Somehow, in some way, some guy was able to break through everyday convention, flag her attention, and take down her telephone number — and perhaps even her panties. It happens all the time. And it's a fantastic way to meet women.

The only trouble is, there's a whole lot of guys who don't think it can be done. They're convinced that "nice girls" just won't turn on to a complete stranger ... that the only way to meet decent women is to get introduced to them at parties and work and dances. They've closed their minds to the fact that buses and street corners and bars and parks and museums are the best places in the whole world to meet the kind of girls they're dying to get their hands on.

Just read what happened to Jane, one of The Fabulous 25. She's a beautiful fashion editor for a woman's magazine and comes from a fine Connecticut banking family.

Jane: My parents'd kill me if they ever found out. But the guy I brought home for the weekend last month was somebody I'd met only the afternoon before in a museum.

We were both looking at this Cezanne and he asked me what I thought of it. Naturally, I said it was great. He said it stunk. I was shocked. Like a sucker, I asked him why. He was a real ugly guy — or so I thought at the time — with wild black hair and tremendous buck teeth.

He gave me some crazy reason why the painting was no good, something about the lines having no balance. I told him he was nuts. We got into this fairly loud argument. It was embarassing. He said if I'd let him buy me coffee at the museum cafeteria he'd prove to me once and for all why the painting was mediocre.

8

But when we finally sat down in the cafeteria he admitted the only reason he said the painting was lousy was to get to talk to me.

I thought it was funny. In fact I was really impressed. We talked for a few minutes and then he asked me if I wanted to see a flick that night. I really didn't feel like it all that much, but I didn't have anything else to do so I said alright. He picked me up at my apartment about nine. I was terrified — not really knowing him at all. But it worked out great.

After the movie we went to this crazy sort of bar for drinks. He was very funny. And suddenly I noticed those huge buck teeth of his were starting to grow on me. There was something very sexy about them. That always happens to me when a guy is really interesting.

After awhile he said let's go back to his apartment. I was a little drunk by this time but I knew what he had in mind. But I said to myself, what the hell. It'll be fun. I'm through not going to bed with a guy I want to go to bed with just because it's not supposed to be "nice." You only live once and I think you ought to have as much fun as you can.

Anyway, we stayed over at his place. Naturally we didn't get much sleep.

The next morning I was supposed to go home for the weekend to visit my parents. But I didn't really feel like leaving this guy. We were sitting there drinking coffee and smoking and it was so nice. So I asked him if he wanted to come out to Connecticut with me. He said sure.

Then I called up my folks and told them I was bringing an old boyfriend along with me, someone I'd dated in college. They were delighted. If they found out the real story they'd go berserk.

It cracks me up.

"SURE, I'D GET PICKED UP!"

It's not surprising that a whole lot of guys in this world think the only way to meet a great woman is to be introduced to her. I used to think the exact same thing. In fact before I started work on this book I never even came close to approaching a strange woman. I was sure if I ever did I'd get bopped on the head with a pocketbook.

Man, was I wrong! Most single women are dying to get picked up. At least that's the concensus of The Fabulous 25:

> *Bonnie:* Any girl will let herself be picked up.

> *Susan:* I have no hard and fast rules. If a man approaches me on the street I'm certainly not going to say, Look, I can't talk to you because I don't know you.

> That would be really dumb. If I like the guy I'll go out with him.

> *Linda:* Of course I get picked up. How else am I going to meet guys?

It makes you wonder. How come women have changed so much? How come they can't wait to get picked up all of a sudden? They weren't always like that.

Well, the answer is sort of complex. But mainly it has to do with changing times. Twenty years ago you would have been right in assuming it was almost impossible to strike up a relationship with a strange girl. But that was twenty years ago. That was before the Pill and disco and see-through blouses and the whole sexual revolution. That was when a good girl wouldn't sleep with you until you grooved that old ring onto her anxious little wedding finger. And when you didn't talk about — you should pardon the expression — "legs" in mixed company.

But things have changed. Now we constantly see movies in which people cavort around nude and talk dirty and make love in living color. And it's influenced our everyday lives.

Suddenly nice girls **are** sleeping with men before they get married. Young modern women are thinking to themselves, "Why should I tell a pleasant, attractive man to get lost if he happens to approach me on the street? No man would do that to a woman. So why should I pretend I don't want to sleep with someone I really do want to sleep with?"

Women are discovering that, just like men, they, too, have a right to act the way they want — that it's madness in this short life of ours to pretend we don't want to do what we really do want to do.

This was reflected in almost everything The Fabulous 25 had to say about picking up. To them it's the 1980's way to meet men ... hip, modern ... purer than a blind date, less artificial than being formally introduced ... in short, more in tune with the way relationships begin these days.

> *Carol:* As far as I'm concerned it's (picking up) the only really decent way to meet people.

> *Connie:* It used to be you'd say to yourself, I'd like to sleep with the guy but that's "bad." Now

you think, there's a guy I'd love to go to bed with. Now how can I get him to notice me? Sleeping with men is fun. And women are finally admitting it to themselves. At least I know I am.

Laura: Being formally introduced to someone through a friend, a party, someone's sister — that's traditional — that was what you did a long time ago.

I couldn't be less interested when someone says, "I have a friend for you." I don't like blind dates. I'd much rather be picked up. I've had bad experiences with blind dates. When you get picked up it's your own choice.

MISS LONELYHEARTS

Did you know that women get lonely? *Very* lonely.

Maybe you never thought about that. Maybe every time you see a good-looking girl stroll by you think to yourself, Gee, she looks happy and secure. I'll bet she's got lots of dates and if I tried to pick her up I'd just be horning in where I'm not really wanted.

Well, if that's what you're thinking, you're out of your mind. Women are fragile, sensitive creatures. And just like you and me, if they're not dating, they get very lonely and depressed. Too many women, even with today's advances, don't have the kind of challenging jobs or golf and tennis and football to keep them busy all day as we do. So they depend much more on deep personal relationships. In short, they depend more on love.

> *Kathy:* Sometimes I feel really down and blue and lonely. If somebody comes along and I can share something with him, like, if I can tell him my problem, that's nice. I really dig that.

> *Linda:* I get lonely lots of times. All women do. We get lonely and bored and trapped in insecure relationships. It's very hard to get a good relationship, one that makes you feel loved and wanted. That's why so many women are always looking to meet new men.

Next time you spot a girl you'd like to pick up don't automatically assume her life is one big glorious orgy of fun and parties and dances. Don't automatically assume

14

she doesn't need you. After all, she may hate the guy she's going out with. Or even worse, she may not be going out with any guy at all.

A good friend of mine was on a business trip a few years ago in, of all places, Peoria, Illinois. Much to his dismay he couldn't get a plane to his home, San Francisco, until the next morning.

That night he went to the best restaurant in town, all by himself. He was miserable.

The hostess in the restaurant was a beautiful woman of about thirty-five. My friend is only twenty-six. Nevertheless, he couldn't take his eyes off the woman. She was tall and slender with high cheek bones and a really friendly smile. He daydreamed of taking her back to his motel room later on but felt that if she wasn't married she certainly had more of a social life than she knew what to do with. He watched her joking and laughing with many of the businessmen who came in for dinner. It never occured to him that she might be bitterly lonely.

Since my friend had nowhere to go later that night, he loafed through dinner, drinking an entire bottle of wine. Then he lingered over a few brandies.

The restaurant began emptying out. The hostess was still there, though,and my friend motioned her over to his table.

"I want to tell you,"he said, "that my dinner was terrific. In fact it was so good I'd like to buy you a brandy."

She smiled politely and said the employees weren't allowed to sit down with the customers.

"C'mon," he urged her. "Just for a short one. No one'll notice."

She looked around. The restaurant was almost completely empty. She sat down.

They sipped brandy and talked ... for hours. Before they knew it it was 1:30. They were both a little drunk.

Suddenly my friend felt the woman looking at him very intently.

"Can I stay with you tonight?" she asked.

He couldn't believe his ears. But of course he wasn't about to turn her down.

They went back to his motel room and made love. There was something urgent and almost desperate about the hostess. She clung to my friend passionately. He really dug it.

Later they sat up and talked. She told him she'd been divorced for about ten years now and had no desire to remarry. It just wasn't for her. Consequently she spent many nights alone. Most of the men in Peoria were married, or thought (like my friend) that she was all booked up. Suddenly my friend understood why she had been so much the aggressor. She just couldn't stand the idea of spending another night alone.

Now whenever my friend has to go to Peoria on business he looks up the beautiful hostess. More often than not, she's free for the evening; and they spend the night together.

STARTING OVER

The statistics on divorce today are mind-boggling. Something like one in every three marriages ends in divorce before three years. Include guys who are separated, and that adds up to a hell of a lot of formerly married guys who are alone ... and lonely.

Getting back into the pick up scene after years of having that one girl to come home to every night can be difficult ... if not downright scary. Picking up is like anything else — to be good at it takes practice. If you don't practice for a couple of years you get rusty So don't be discouraged if your first night at a local singles bar isn't all you'd dreamed it would be. You'll probably need some time to get reacquainted with the singles atmosphere and to see what changes have come about since you were in the fray last. Go out those first couple times like you're a student of picking up, a casual observer. Think of yourself as the Gay Talese of your home town. This attitude will take some of the pressure off yourself and before long you'll get the hang of it again and be picking up girls all over the place.

There are also a few general pointers worth remembering:

1. *Be patient.* The biggest problem for guys who are recently divorced or separated is impatience ... they can't wait even one week for a new girl. They are so used to having a warm body next to them in bed night after night, it's just something they take for granted. Some divorced guys think their organ's going to shrivel up and drop off if they don't use it everyday. Well, that ain't true.

17

Even though it's difficult, don't give in to the temptation of demanding a woman's body and throwing yourself upon her. Desperation looks bad on a man and nine times out of ten you'll scare the girl off. Be cool, be patient. The rewards are not far off.

2. *Act your age.* I met a very attractive 30 year old female divorcee who told me about a party she went to for divorced and separated singles. She was dying to get out and meet a nice guy, someone to talk to and hug and hold (she admitted to feeling quite horny). When she got to the party there were plenty of guys there but they were all packed together in a corner of the room guzzling beers. Every one of them was either too shy, too scared or too insecure to move from the group and mingle. They stayed in the corner telling dirty jokes and getting drunk ... a gangling, giggling group of "teenagers". The women stood around talking to one another, eyeing the men, and getting lonelier by the minute. My friend said that if just one reasonably mature, interesting guy broke from the pack she would have thrown herself upon him and taken him home to bed. But it didn't happen. She went home lonely, frustrated and *still* very horny.

The point of this little anecdote is obvious. You may be single again, but you're *not* seventeen again. Act your age when you're meeting new women and you'll have much better luck with them.

3. *Be confident.* A lot of divorced and separated guys think they're at a disadvantage because they feel their divorced status carries an awful stigma. Others worry that they're not as young as they used to be and therefore can't compete with 20 year old men making the singles circuit. Neither of these things is true. Statis-

tics bear out that every year there are more and more singles in their 30's, 40's and even in their 50's. The singles scene is getting older than it was fifteen years ago, and no one is at a disadvantage because of it. Fifty year old guys are out there picking up twenty-five year old girls just as successfully as younger guys and, in many cases, more successfully.

Remember that for every divorced or separated guy, there is a divorced or separated girl. That means you have an excellent chance of meeting hundreds of women every day in exactly the same shoes you're in. There is no stigma attached to divorce or separation like there used to be, and you're at no disadvantage with women if you are divorced. In fact, many women who are recently divorced or separated feel more comfortable with men in the same situation. So you actually have the upper hand with these women over other guys.

There are also very few single women who are put off by divorced men. For one thing divorce is such a common occurrence today (you are one of tens of millions) women just naturally expect to meet divorced men. There are also a lot of women who, for various reasons, prefer a man who has already been married. For one thing he is usually more mature than a lot of young guys running around in singles bars ... and women find maturity very appealing. Divorced men are also likely to be established in a career, which means job security, which means more money. But probably the biggest attraction for women to divorced men can be summarized in one word ... *sex.* A man who's been married has had *a lot of sex.* He's experienced, he's knowledgeable, he knows how to satisfy. And this is very, very sexy to a woman.

When you return to the singles scene don't overlook the places created especially for you. Divorced singles clubs, parties, cruises, and singles bars and restaurants that cater to a slightly older crowd are great places for you to get back into the swing of things. These places are not filled with losers and nerds. They are filled with people like you who are looking for fun, excitement and companionship. It doesn't matter how old you are, there is always someone there for you. And you don't have to be concerned about telling a woman you're divorced, because she already knows it.

Try coed health clubs too. Singles are always interested in looking good and keeping a youthful appearance so they flock to health clubs. If you're not an exercise nut yourself don't worry about it. Most fitness clubs are created to serve a social function anyway so you won't feel like an oddball if ten pushups is all you can handle.

If you're about to change your address anyway take a little extra time to search out an apartment complex that is heavily inhabited by singles. There is no better place to meet a single woman than as her neighbor within the confines of her home territory. She's not likely to feel threatened by a neighbor and she'll be a lot more relaxed and comfortable, so you'll have little trouble getting to know her.

Starting over does not have to be difficult or frightening. You are at *no* disadvantage either if you're divorced or separated. In fact, you may be just what most women are looking for.

WHEN YOU CAN'T FIND A PLAYBOY CENTERFOLD ...

Everywhere you look, whether it be in newspapers or magazines or on t.v., there's a gorgeous girl telling you that all you have to do to get a girl like her is to wear a certain cologne, drink a particular brand of scotch, or drive a certain type of car. These ads work well to sell products, but rarely do the products get the girl. We've been so brainwashed by the media to think that the most desirable girls are also (and only) the most physically attractive, that sometimes we won't even look twice at a relatively attractive girl and certainly not at a genuinely homely one. But there's a lot to be said for the girls who aren't the obvious beauties.

Now don't get me wrong. I love beautiful women, too, and I'm not going to tell you to abandon your dreams of getting a date with the hottest-looking girl in town. But if you're smart, you won't easily overlook the real advantages of the average girl.

First of all, I've found that a lot of beautiful women are really up-tight about being approached since many of them have always been treated as so-called "sex-objects". A lot of these girls freeze as soon as a guy walks up to them — they're hardly a barrel of laughs on a date.

Another thing I've discovered over the years is that all those incredible girls you see in Playboy and Penthouse every month aren't so incredible in the flesh. I'll never forget the time one of the big modeling agencies in New York sent me photographs of several girls I was thinking of using on the cover of this book. They were really stunning ... I could hardly wait to meet them. For a week after getting those photographs I wouldn't give a second look to the girls in the small town where I lived. Finally I decided which model I wanted to use and I arranged to meet her. She walked into my office and I thought she was a girl looking for the employment agency down the street. I literally didn't recognize her. Where was the perfect piece of ass I saw in the photo from the agency? I've learned since then that make-up, lighting, and a good photographer, go a long way to create that perfect picture. Sure she was pretty, but really not much prettier than a lot of the girls I saw everyday. Heck, I realized that many of the girls in my home town could look just as good as those high-priced models with a little primping ... even better.

A woman who is not beautiful by ordinary standards can still be beautiful. If you can forget about the magazine models for a second and really take a long look at a girl who doesn't instantly knock you off your feet, you'll probably find there are some very appealing things about her. She also may seem a lot less up-tight about being approached.

Another thing you'll find is that a lot of regular-looking girls *become* beautiful as you get to know them. You know the old saying about beauty being in the eyes of the beholder? Well, it's really true. I've met a lot of women whose looks did not impress me at first; but when I got to know them, when we began to share feelings and intimacies and experiences, they really became beautiful. Their appearance didn't change, but the way I saw them did. They became beautiful to me.

Outward beauty has little to do with how good a time you have with a girl. A lot of guys will tell you that the most beautiful girls are the hardest to loosen up and have fun with. Either they're obsessed with their looks and terribly vain, or they're scared to death that you're just using them. Whatever the reason, it's often the "unobvious" beauty who turns out to be the most fun, both in and out of bed. Girls who aren't classic beauties are less likely to depend on their looks to carry them through a relationship. Instead, tenderness and a desire to please become their strong points, and those are both hard things to resist.

In the long run you'll probably find that spending years searching for that Playboy centerfold is useless, because few girls, if any, look that way in real life. In fact, you don't have to look much farther than our own home town, your school, or your office to find a girl who's both genuinely beautiful in her own special way and very willing to start a relationship with you.

So get out and get into all the marvelous girls walking around who may not be stunning beauties, but who'll make it up a thousand times over in affection and loving. And with a little caring from you, you may find that these very same girls blossom into great beauties. A girl's beauty is like a flower's. Without caring and nurturing the flower wilts. But give it water and sun and tenderness and it suddenly becomes spectacularly beautiful. Give a girl a little confidence, give her some loving, and suddenly her natural good looks bloom, too, right before your eyes. You have the power to bring that out in a girl ... any girl. So why wait ... go find a girl and make her beautiful.

WOMEN GET HORNY

Do you know that women get just as horny as you do? Well, it's true. They sit home, all by themselves, and think how terrific it would feel to hop into bed with some-one. Anyone. Just to relieve their horniness.

> *Diane:* I'm going to be very frank with you. A few months ago I hadn't gone out with a man for a long time. I was very horny. In fact I was dying to get laid. Really. If a nice man had approached me I would have gone up to his room and right to bed with him. It's a shame no one approached me.

Does that shock you? It shouldn't. Women have come a long way recently. They're learning they have the same right to sexual freedom that men have. In fact I think it's going to be harder for men to adjust to the sexual revolu-tion than it is for women.

> *Janet:* Sure, women get horny. Sometimes I go home and read a sexy book because I don't have a sexy man around.

> *Mary:* What men don't seem to realize is that most girls are looking for a good sexual rela-tionship just as hard as they are. If a man is honest and sincere and shows an interest in me as a woman, then I feel like having sex with him. And if I feel like it, I do.

You see, women have *strong* sexual urges, after all. They love sex just like *you* do. And if they don't have it for awhile — especially if they've gotten used to it — it makes them horny.

So next time you're wondering whether to try to pick up a certain girl, remember: It may be a long time since she's been to bed with a man. She may be horny. Very horny. Right at that very moment.

And maybe, just by saying hello to her, you'll be the lucky guy she decides to relieve her frustrations on.

Photo by Jon Agnello

25

TALK DIRTY

In the last chapter we talked about girls getting horny. Now we're going to discuss something intimately related with that: Talking dirty. One of the best, and very possibly *the* best technique for picking up women and then seducing them, is to talk dirty to them.

What do I mean by "talking dirty?" Simply this: Freely sprinkling your conversation with words of sex. Letting women know verbally that you're a pretty sexy guy. Women love it. I know this may sound insane ... but it's true. Any great lover knows it for a fact.

Of course, most girls will never admit to liking crude men. Many of them even pretend to be offended by sexy talk. But that's just a front. If you didn't titillate them with talk of making love to them, they'd probably be bored out of their minds.

I asked a close female friend why this is so. She said, "Because women are dirty-minded. They're just as sex-obsessed as men are. The only difference is, women don't have enough outlets. It's okay for men to leer at women's bodies all day long. But women can't do that. At least not so openly. So when they do get the chance to engage in sex play, even if it's only conversational, they love it. It arouses them."

Like we discovered in the last chapter, women get horny. And when you talk dirty to them, it stimulates that horniness.

Think of it this way. If a woman told you you had a sexy walk or sensual shoulders or great legs, it'd really turn you on. Well, girls are just as much sexual creatures as men are. Why do you think they wear skintight jeans and low cut, slinky blouses? Why do you think so many of them have completely stopped wearing bras and panties? Just to look pretty? Don't be crazy. They're showing you their breasts and behinds to *stimulate* you. To make you want to go to bed with them. Because every girl knows if her body is packaged well, you'll try to pick her up.

Not too long ago a friend of mine was passing a bookstore in Denver, Colorado. He spotted a young girl in the window, arranging a display of bestsellers. The girl had an incredibly provocative slit up the back of her skirt, and was leaning further and further over trying to arrange the books just so.

Consequently her skirt revealed more and more of her legs. My friend happily prepared himself to see what he *thought* was going to be her panties. But he got way more than he bargained for. The girl wasn't wearing any panties at all, only an absolutely transparent pair of pantyhose. He could see her entire bare ass ... and it just so happened to be a great one. He stayed and watched for about three glorious minutes until the girl finished her window display and hopped back into the interior of the store.

The next day my friend stopped by the bookstore, pretending to be looking for a hard-to-find novel. Needless to say, he selected the girl with the beautiful behind to help him. She turned out to be just as good-looking from the front as she was from the rear. While she was turning the store upside-down looking for my friend's book, they started talking. About literature and the weather and a great new record album she'd just bought. After a few minutes it only seemed natural that my friend ask her if she wanted to have lunch. She said sure.

He took her to a dark, intimate little restaurant. After a few drinks, and completely on impulse, he told her about his first view of her. She blushed a little and giggled.

"I'm really glad you don't wear underpants," he said, "because otherwise I wouldn't have got to see the nicest ass I've ever seen — in my entire life."

The girl was delighted. That afternoon they both called in sick, checked into a hotel, and spent the rest of the day making love.

The point of this story is not that the girl was "bad" or "fast" or "avant garde." All it indicates is that normal, healthy young females like sex. Want sex. And, most important of all, will be glad to have sex with you if you only ask them.

But I'm getting off the subject. We were discussing talking dirty to women. And here's an important little *warning.* Not *all* women will respond to your talking dirty to them with a violent sexual passion. Some of them have to be warmed up first. And others are prudes who no one can warm up. Which means you have to be somewhat discriminating how fast and with whom you start talking sexy. You have to use a little finesse.

But don't let this stop you. The rewards are far greater than the risks. Being sexy and provocative with women really turns them on. It gets them *excited* about you.

Don't be a goody-goody. It doesn't work. Don't talk like a Sunday school teacher. You'll only impress nuns and girls' mothers. Not the girls themselves.

Women are constantly intrigued by sex. In fact, more than anything else you could talk to them about. So let them know *you're* thinking about it, too. Let them know you're a very sexy guy.

Otherwise, they just might assume you're not particularly interested in sex. And they won't be interested in you.

So talk dirty. Believe me, you'll get slapped a lot less often than you think. And get it on with a lot more women.

JUST ASK

This suggestion is as useful in life as it is for picking up girls. The point is this — you get what you want when you ask for it. As nice as it would be, women just don't walk into a bar, sweep you into their arms, and take you back to their apartments. If you want to meet a girl and start a relationship with her you've got to ask for it.

The great thing about asking (for her name, her number, if she wants to dance, join you for a drink, etc.) is that more often than not it releases a torrent of conversation. And conversation leads to familiarity which leads to the best kind of relationships.

One type of question you can ask a girl that always gets a response is for advice. Every woman is born with a natural instinct to advise. They love the feeling that they're nurturing and caring for you. It gives them that motherly feeling of importance.

You can ask advice about anything, but preferably something she knows a little about. Ask how long you should marinate shish-kabab; and after she tells you, ask her to join you for this exotic meal. Ask her if she knows a good French restaurant in the neighborhood — one where the two of you can share a bottle of wine. Ask her if she has a good remedy for a stiff neck. This is an especially good one since she'll probably offer to rub the pain away. Ask anything that gives her the opportunity to offer some advice.

Asking a girl for a date, her telephone number or even her name can be a little frightening at times, but rarely is it as awful as we make it out in our fantasies. And think of the times you walked away from a girl you couldn't take your eyes off of because you didn't ask ... you left her there never knowing if maybe she wasn't the dynamite girl who was going to flip over you, if she wasn't the girl who was going to change your life.

Keep this in mind: If you don't ask you'll never know. You'll never know if that cute blonde at the bakery will go to the movies with you Friday night; you'll never know if that shapely brunette in your math class has the same passion for ice cream as you do; you'll never know if that athletic-looking redhead in the accounting department wants to join you for a bike ride in the park.

Asking is the key. You'll find that just the act of asking can be half or even the whole battle when you're trying to pick up a girl. Because most women want nothing more than for you to give them the opportunity to say yes. And if you can ask, you'll discover a world of attractive, desirable women everyday who are looking for companionship just as much as you are.

If I discovered anything by talking to the Fabulous 25 it's this: *Give a girl a chance and she'll help you pick her up.*

DO YOU MEAN BUSINESS?

One question you have to ask yourself about picking up girls is, Do you *really* want to pick them up? If you met a great-looking girl on your way to work and she said, "I really like you. Let's go somewhere and make love," would you be willing to forget about everything and instantly check into the nearest hotel with her?

If your answer is a resounding, "Yes!" then you have a lot going for you. A woman will sense you mean business and it'll turn her on. Why? Because a woman is a very cautious creature. She doesn't want to be hurt. Before she makes any sort of commitment to you she wants to be damn sure you're going to take her up on it. Nothing enrages her more than when a man, who's already made a pass at her, backs down at the last moment. It makes her feel like a fool.

One of the best picker uppers I know is a guy named Peter — he'd drop anything to pick up a girl. When he puts the make on a woman she knows he means business. His Aunt Milly could be on her deathbed, yet if he found a willing young woman on the way to the hospital I don't have to tell you which lady's room he'd wind up in.

When it comes to picking up girls Peter is tireless, his every action inspired. I am in awe of his talents. He has that extra desire, that special drive, to pursue a pick up to the very end, no matter where it leads him — his room, her room, the corner motel, even the golf course. And the women he goes after sense this from the start. But they aren't frightened away or put off by his enthusiasm. On the contrary, they love it. It makes them feel important, sexy, like there is no one else in the world he'd rather be with. They open up to him because they know he isn't going to suddenly cop out on them.

You might find this surprising, but an awful lot of guys only *think* they want to pick up girls. If any girl actually took them up on their offer they'd invent some excuse to run home to mother. That's why you have a tremendous advantage over many other guys if you're really serious about picking up. The more a girl senses you mean business, the easier it is to pick her up.

Think about that. The very fact that you're dead serious about wanting to pick up women can be a far more valuable talent than super good looks or great wit and charm.

LOOKS

Just how good-looking do you have to be to pick up women? Do you need the proverbial square jaw ... the dazzling blue eyes ... the lean, hard, six-foot frame?

The answer, quite simply, is *no.* Believe it or not, looks are only secondary when it comes to picking up girls.

Now I know damn well this may sound like a lot of bullcrap. The thing is, it just so happens to be the truth. Men find this hard to believe because to a man a woman's looks are of *paramount* importance. But women are different from men. They really are. They're much more interested in what a man is like on the inside than the outside.

Before I talked to The Fabulous Twenty-Five I thought good looks were tremendously important ... that without them a man didn't stand a chance. But read what the girls have to say and you'll see how incredibly mistaken I was.

> *Monique:* Actually, I *prefer* men who aren't very good-looking. They have better personalities. They're more interesting. They have more flare. They don't sit back and depend on their looks. In the long run, they're far more exciting.

> *Mary:* To me a man's looks are completely irrelevant.

Ruth: A man's looks aren't worth a damn if he isn't warm and interesting. And if he's warm and interesting then I don't give a damn what he looks like.

All this, of course, isn't to say that it won't help if you happen to be very handsome. A great-looking man *does* catch a woman's eye. But when all is said and done, a woman is way more interested in a man's personality then in his face or build. Women just aren't hung up on beautiful faces the same way men are.

Millions of guys would marry a low-grade moron if she had the looks and figure of a Vegas chorus girl. But women don't work the same way. Not at all.

Gail: If a guy approaches me in a nice way then I'm always willing to hear what he has to say. I have to hear a man open his mouth first before I decide whether I dig his looks or not. As far as I'm concerned, he doesn't have to be anywhere near an Adonis. If I like the way he talks and what he has to say then I'm intrigued.

Susan: I react to a person — not his looks. If a very good-looking guy approaches me, but I don't particularly like him, then I no longer find him especially attractive.

On the other hand, a guy who isn't especially attractive can really start looking good if he gets me interested in what he has to say. If he seems like a nice, interesting person.

BEAUTY AND THE BEAST

Speaking of looks, I'd like to tell you about Tom, a very ugly friend of mine. He's a hip, witty guy, but, man, is he ugly! He himself refers to his face as a sort of a cross between a kindly gorilla and a sophisticated, middle-aged toad.

Tom's looks, though, didn't keep him from marrying Laura — one of the loveliest brunettes I've ever seen.

It all happened about three years ago. Tom was working as a swimming instructor at an all-boys' camp somewhere in the Berkshire Mountains.

He'd expected the summer to be a blast. The owner of the camp had filled his head with visions of nearby girls' camps where luscious female counselors were known to rape swimming instructors on sight.

This proved not to be the case. In fact after four weeks up in those mountains Tom hadn't even *seen* a girl. He was growing more and more lonely and bored. The cool, starry country nights were just made for loving. But he didn't have the slightest idea where to find someone to love.

On one of his rare nights off Tom borrowed a car and drove into Pittsfield, the nearest town of any size. It was about eleven, and the streets were deserted.

Tom walked past the town's only movie theatre. It was just letting out. In the crowd leaving the theatre he spotted a sensational-looking girl of about nineteen or twenty. She was with her parents.

Getting up all his courage, Tom walked up to the family and asked if they knew of a nice snackbar anywhere around. They happened to be going for ice cream sodas themselves and told Tom to follow them in his car.

When Tom walked into the ice cream parlor, the family was already seated at a table. Tom looked over at them longingly, hoping they'd invite him to join them. But they just waved hello and went back to their sodas. So Tom sat down all by himself at the counter. I'm probably too ugly for them, he told himself. My face would spoil their appetites. But when he looked up from his banana split a little later he caught the girl staring at him. She blushed and quickly looked away.

Damn! If only she were alone, Tom thought. Then I'd try to pick her up. But then he thought of his job. And how he had nearly half the summer left up in those lonely, boring mountains. If he didn't find a girl soon he'd go stark, raving mad. Parents or not, he decided, here goes!

He stood up and walked over to their table. "Listen," he said, "I know this is going to sound crazy, but I've been trapped as a swimming teacher at a boys' camp for the past month and I'm going out of my mind with boredom. If I don't talk to some non-camp people soon I'm going to drown at least nine of my campers. You can help save their lives by inviting me to join you."

They seemed delighted to have Tom join them. In fact they even apologized for not having invited him over.

They were really a lovely family. The girl's father

was a professor of biology at Princeton. Her mother was a violinist. She was a junior at New York University. They owned a lake house a few miles away and were spending the summer there.

Tom and the girl hit it off right away. He really enjoyed talking with her. After a half hour or so her parents said they were going home to bed. "Would you mind driving Claire back?" they asked. Mind? Tom could barely keep himself from leaping onto the table and breaking into a mad dance of joy.

He and the girl went to a roadside bar for a few drinks. Besides her fantastic looks, there was something very nice about her. She had a certain kind of soft, feminine hipness - not too giggly, not too brash. Just right.

Claire told Tom what a drag the summer had become. At first if was nice doing nothing ... lounging in the sun. But now she was bored. She admitted how glad she was they'd met.

When Tom drove her home she invited him in. They necked for awhile. Tom put his hand under her blouse. She wasn't wearing any bra. He nearly fainted from pleasure. Still, she wouldn't let him sleep with her.

"Look," she told him, "I really dig you. You're funny. You're nice. I want to see you again. Soon. And if I don't screw for you I know damn well you'll be back — if only to sleep with me. Pretty smart, huh?" She smiled.

He had to agree, it was pretty smart. He knew he'd be back.

And he was. Every single night he could get off. Soon they were sleeping together. And still Tom kept on coming back. There was something about the girl that had really got to him. And apparently there was something about Tom — who knows, maybe it was his very ugliness — that had reached the girl.

When the summer was over they kept on seeing each other. A few months later they were married.

If you happened to see their wedding picture you'd probably ask yourself, What in God's name did she ever see in him?

It's a real case of beauty and the beast.

A GOOD PERSONALITY

The first thing a man looks for in a woman is good looks and sexiness. The first thing a woman looks for in a man is a good *personality.* Not the "personality" you probably associate with the mid-fifties — the bubbly, corny bounciness of the "personality kid" in the white bucks and cheer-leader sweater.

Today when a woman says personality she's talking about a special kind of warmth and humanity and honesty she wants in a man, a kind of gentle masculinity that makes her feel womanly and wanted.

> *Diane:* If a man is human and interesting, that's all I ask. I don't give a damn what he looks like. But I *do* give a damn about how he thinks and acts and talks.

> *Connie:* I've come to find men attractive who at first gave me the chills I thought they were so ugly. It's amazing how many times this has happened to me.

41

CUTE FEET

Just what do women find sexually stimulating about men? You'd be amazed!

Women are nuts. They really are. They're totally unpredictable.

If a group of guys standing on the corner spots a girl with a gorgeous face and a deliciously curvy behind, they all go crazy and elbow each other in the ribs.

Women don't work that way at all. They are far more individual in their tastes. There's no telling what any given woman will find sexy about any given man. Men tend to flip over things like breasts and faces and legs. Women go crazy over little things ... things you wouldn't expect. Some of The Fabulous 25 said that if a man had the right kind of hands he could have carte blanche with them. A famous psychiatrist wrote about a girl who found shapely hands "irresistibly" attractive in men.

Other women get turned on by eyes and noses and freckles. Still others don't care what a man looks like so long as he has a nice smile.

There's really no figuring it out. A friend of mine once slept with a beautiful girl he met at the beach simply because she flipped over his feet. His *feet,* mind you. She told him about it the next morning in bed.

"You know why I let you pick me up yesterday on the beach?" she asked. "Because you've got the sexiest, cutest feet I've ever seen."

Here he'd been breaking his neck for years trying to be a great success with women, not realizing that all he really had to do was walk around with his shoes off.

It all leads to one overwhelming conclusion: *You* may not consider yourself the handsomest cat in town. But there may be a thousand great girls out there who think you have sensational eyelashes or dynamite teeth or fantastic cheekbones. So don't get all neurotic and insecure because you're not the spitting image of Richard Gere. Without realizing it, you may have some incredible feature that will literally drive women wild.

> *Bonnie:* I don't know what turns me on about men, but it has nothing to do with whether they're bad-looking or good-looking because even ugly guys appeal to me for some reason. Maybe it's because I like the way they wear their hair or the way their pants fit. Not the clothes, but the fit of them. Or maybe it's their hands or their whole appearance. Most of the guys I really flip for aren't anywhere near good-looking according to traditional standards.

HOW TO BE SEXY

What makes a man sexy?

According to our Fabulous 25 one of the most important ingredients is length of hair. The quarter-inch Marine crew cut *will* turn heads ... in the other direction. And the shoulder length "campus radical" style so popular during the 60's is equally unattractive to women today. **Without exception** each of the Fabulous 25 said she prefers men with moderately long hair.

If you're having trouble picking a style, or finding the look that's "you", go to a good hair stylist and for $15 they'll give you a great hair-cut that women will admire. And no matter what kind of hair quality you have, an experienced stylist can fashion the right look for you. Remember, according to the Fabulous 25, good-looking hair is dynamite.

What else gives a man lots of sex appeal. Some of the girls said it helps to act aloof and cold. Of course, that's a little difficult when you're trying to pick someone up. After all, it's *you* who's approaching *them.* That alone says you're interested.

What I think the girls mean by "aloof" is that you should maintain a certain reserve. Don't throw yourself at a girl's feet right away. Don't grovel. Don't come on with, "Oh, I need you so much. I worship the ground you walk on." With crap like that the ground she'll walk on will be you.

Be friendly and polite. But keep your dignity. Don't go all to pieces just because you're talking to a pretty girl. After all, there are *millions* of pretty girls in the world.

What else will make you sexy? Experiment. When you find something that works you'll know it from the way women start looking at you. Try on some new, fashionable clothes ... whatever the style is. Be dramatic, be daring. Unbutton your shirt a little lower. Wear tight pants or a mysterious pair of shades. *Think* sexy. Think, I am a virile male animal. If I made love to that cute girl over there, she'd get weak in the knees.

> *Harriet:* Nobody likes a guy who's apologetic about his very existence. If a guy acts like he's worth something, like he *knows* he's sexy, then half his battle's over. I'll automatically assume he really is worth something.

Here's the most important thing the Fabulous Twenty-Five said about being sexy. If you're interesting, don't hide it. Bring the fascinating real you up to the surface.

If you play the bass guitar, or even if you're the world's greatest living authority on the mating habits of frogs, let your lady friends know about it. If you run a quarter mile in forty-eight seconds, you're not the only one who finds it interesting. Girls dig accomplishment. To them it's sexy.

Let the real you emerge. Don't *hide* your best features. *Advertise* them.

It's absolutely not true that a girl can take one look at you and know all about you. What you think. What you're

45

really like inside. What you do for a living. What's interesting and exciting about you. You've got to *tell* her all about you. *That* is sexy.

You may know how great and witty and brilliant and *sensual* you are.

But she won't unless you tell her.

> *Alix:* If a guy's really interesting, he could look like a gorilla and still be very sexy. It's as simple as that.

THE WORLD'S GREATEST PICKUP TECHNIQUE

Now we're going to get down to the real nitty gritty of picking up women: The Approach. What you actually say and do to pick girls. The very words to use when you first approach them.

The first and most important thing you should know about the different approaches is that none can rival just plain being yourself. This is the greatest technique of all.

You're a pretty important person. You're interesting, sensitive, kind, manly, and you dig women. And that's plenty. The more you adjust to being "plain old You" the more successful you'll be with the ladies you meet.

If you're not the wittiest guy in the world, then don't try to be a Steve Martin. It won't look right on you.

If you're not a big business tycoon, then don't flash around a big wad of bills. You'll look phony and pretentious. Just be yourself. For most women, that's the most extraordinary and wonderful quality of all.

Any man with the guts and pride to be proud of who and what he really is is bound to turn on women.

> *Mary:* A man doesn't have to be anything other than himself. Most guys try to be something they aren't in order to make an impression. But I'm most impressed by a friendly, complimentary guy who is just being himself.

Lisa: Last year a minister picked me up right on the street in New York City. A young minister, about thirty years old. I was walking to my local deli for some cornflakes and he stopped me and asked if I knew of any apartments for rent in the area.

We started talking and he started walking with me and we stopped and had a cup of coffee. And then we started dating. We went out together for over a year. And the thing I'll always remember about him, the thing that really impressed me, was his naturalness. Even when he first approached me. He didn't try to impress me or snow me. He was himself … and he seemed very happy to be himself. It was nice.

Take all this in carefully. Because it's the most important thing there is to know about picking up girls.

I have a friend who is neither terribly handsome nor rich nor successful nor even good with words. But somehow he turns on more women than just about anyone I know.

How does he do it? Because he likes himself. He feels that the very fact that he's a pleasant, decent human being means that he's worth other people's time and affection.

Women take to him as if he were an All-Pro quarterback. Yet that doesn't surprise him. He automatically expects to be liked. Not in an obnoxious, conceited way. But friendly and openly.

He doesn't worry that he should be taller or thinner or better-looking. He makes no apologies. He simply approaches a woman warmly and pleasantly. And women love him for it.

Next time you approach a girl just try being yourself. It's the greatest technique of all.

RELAX

Another important thing in picking up girls is to be relaxed. Do not, if at all possible, get uptight. You are not on a bombing mission over enemy territory. You're not hunting bull elephants. You are simply going to talk to a woman. That is all.

If she chooses to ignore you, you'll still wind up alive and well. It's not a matter of life and death.

If she hollers on you, you will survive.

If she calls you nasty names, you will *still* survive.

If she hits you with her pocketbook, you may even be able to sue her.

Even if you bungle things terribly and make an incredible fool of yourself, ten minutes later you'll still be able to sit down and enjoy a big steak dinner. In fact, ten minutes later you'll still be able to approach another girl.

The point is, rejection is only *temporary.* The very worst thing that can happen is that you'll get your feelings hurt a little. And, brother, if you can't take that in this world, you're in trouble.

I don't mean to sound harsh or unsympathetic. But getting your feelings hurt occasionally is part of life. You've got to learn to live with it.

Look what happened to me. When I first began

trying to pick up girls I bombed out a lot. And it hurt. But an hour later I was always ready to try again. That's how slight the damage was!

Maybe you can benefit some from my failures. After all, if you get rejected you can always tell yourself you're not alone. The *author* of a book on how to pick up girls was rejected more times than he can remember. And he's lived to talk about it.

Maybe getting rejected isn't as degrading or embarrassing or as disturbing as you think.

> *Lisa:* I wish guys wouldn't get so uptight about trying to pick me up. I want to meet men as much as they want to meet me. It's a very natural thing for strangers to want to talk and show interest in each other. So why get an ulcer over it.

IF YOU CAN'T RELAX

What happens if you can't relax ... if every time you contemplate picking up a girl, your teeth begin to chatter like castinets?

Well, then don't relax. Stay uptight. Oddly enough, it may be the best thing you have going for you. I know this sounds crazy. But it just so happens to be true. Almost half the girls I interviewed said they like shy, awkward guys. When a man approaches them in an awkward, nervous manner, it makes *them* feel less nervous and awkward.

> *Monique:* I like a guy to be a little shy ... a little unaggressive. Otherwise he seems too flippant, like he's not really interested in *me* — but simply saw a good-looking girl he'd like to make. I feel safer if somebody is honestly a little bit reticent.

> *Alice:* When I'm getting picked up, I know I'm getting picked up. And the guy who's picking me up knows it, too. Still, I'd rather not have it be that obvious. So if a guy's a little shy and not that smooth, it makes it all seem more spontaneous ... more innocent. I like it better that way.

To be honest, I don't really understand why so many women work this way. Maybe it's because guys who are shy seem boyish and cute. Maybe it makes women want to mother and cuddle them.

All I can say for sure is that in a hell of a lot of cases it can help to be nervous and awkward. You don't have to be the slickest thing this side of a used car salesman. You don't have to be brimming with confidence. You *can* say dumb things and hem and haw and trip over your tongue and still succeed. Almost despite yourself. In fact you might even do better that way.

> *Diane:* If a guy is too confident and aggressive when he approaches me it's frightening. It's unnatural. It makes me feel like he picks up girls for a living.

ONLY YOU, BABY,
CAN THRILL ME LIKE YOU DO

Here's something you've **got** to know when you're out on the prowl: The woman you're approaching must be made to feel you're head over heels in love with her. This can mean the difference between miraculous success and miserable failure.

For some strange reason, women just can't stand it if they think the only reason you're trying to pick them up is because you happen to find them pretty or pleasant-looking. That's not enough. Not by a long shot. Women don't want to be thought of as just "another pretty girl." They dream of being Cleopatra — someone so enchanting, so maddeningly sexy, wild horses couldn't keep you away.

This need was expressed in interview after interview after interview with The Fabulous Twenty-Five. Frankly, it seems a little naive to me. After all, you probably see fifty girls each day you'd be more than delighted to dive into bed with. But that doesn't mean you've fallen deeply in love with them. True love takes a little more time.

Nevertheless, just about any girl you meet is willing to believe, in fact, is dying to believe, that something about her is so overpowering, so unbelievably out of the ordinary, that you simply could not keep yourself from approaching her.

> **Diane:** I can't feel that I'm just a body to be used, just another girl to chalk up. When a man

approaches me I've got to get the feeling he wants more out of me than a quick lay. He's got to make me feel like an individual. I've got to be me and I want to be important.

Helen: I can't stand it if I get the feeling that five minutes later the guy who's trying to pick me up will be using the exact same pitch on someone else. He's got to really want *me*.

Now you know damn well that the way these girls would like you to feel is not necessarily the way you're going to feel. Half the time you want to pick up a girl it's because she's got a body that makes you dizzy. Or the face of a movie star. Or the hips of a belly dancer. Not because she has some magnetic inner quality. Or whatever the hell it is she wants you to flip over.

But you can't let them know that. You've got to pretend otherwise. And one great way of doing that is to act as if you're completely new to the pick up game ... as if the only reason you're trying it this time is because the girl is so sensational you didn't even know what you were doing.

Laura: If a man doesn't appear embarrassed when he tries to pick me up, I mean if he seems too slick and talented at it, then I assume he does this sort of thing millions of times a day. But if he's a little awkward, as if he's new to it, then I feel better. I don't want to be one of many.

Harriet: When a man tries to pick me up, and he isn't too obvious about it, then I get the feeling it was something special about me that made him overcome his shyness and break out of his shell and talk to me. I figure he saw me and just couldn't resist me.

What these girls are trying to say, men, is that they don't want to get picked up by a professional picker upper. So if you're not a professional, then terrific. You'll bumble around a little, you'll do silly, awkward things, and you'll wind up picking up every woman in sight.

Now what do you do if you are a professional? Disguise the fact. Say things like, "I don't do this very often, but you're so beautiful I just had to come up and talk to you."

Or, "I've never done this in my life before. But there's just something about your eyes that makes me want to know you."

With lines like these you'll make girls feel that it was something exceedingly special about them that made you overcome your shyness and inertia to approach them.

> *Jane:* A man should be sort of polite, you know, maybe like he's almost embarrassed about it, even if inwardly he might not be. If he's embarrassed it's a good indication that he was so struck by me that he couldn't help but come up and speak to me. I'd really be thrilled by that.

DON'T BE NASTY

There's a dumb myth going around that if you're tough and mean and ornery like Bogey (or, at least, the way he was in his flicks), women will throw themselves at your feet.

That ain't true!

Women like men who are nice — that is, men who are **confident** enough to be nice.

Some men act mean because they're afraid of rejection. They'll say something nasty to a girl. And then, when she tells them to get lost, they have an excuse: "I wasn't really trying to pick up that ugly broad anyway," they'll tell themselves. "I was just giving her a hard time for a little fun. For a few laughs."

According to The Fabulous Twenty-Five (and according to good old common sense, too), acting mean for no reason at all is just about the most stupid and destructive thing you could do. Women like men who are nice much more than they like men who are not nice. Sure, there are a few masochistic women around who enjoy being treated like dogs. But the great majority of girls much prefer being treated like queens.

Being warm and friendly and gracious can be one of the greatest techniques there is for picking up women. Even if you're basically not a nice guy to begin with!

Figure it this way. When you approach a woman on a street corner or a bus, it's just as tough for her as it is for you. Not only does she have to deal with the usual awkwardness of meeting a stranger, but she's also got to decide, in a split second, whether you're a mad rapist or not. If, at the same time all this is going on, you say something very charming like, "Boy, are you short!" or, "Your skirt's too long," you're really going to turn her off.

Think of a woman as being somewhat like an ice cube. She has to be melted. And if you want to be the one who gets anywhere with her, then you've got to supply the warmth that will melt her. So, be warm. Be pleasant. Be charming. If you act like a cold, rude bastard, you'll just make her colder and icier.

> *Linda:* I don't go for a man who approaches me with something like, "Gee, you're pretty old to be wearing braces." That I could easily do without. I'd much rather have him talk about my good points.

> *Jennifer:* Basically, women are a pretty insecure group of people. I know I am. I like to feel loved. In fact, I need to feel loved. Otherwise I just won't open up.

> If a guy's really nice to me, then I won't think he's trying to get something off me. I'll think he really likes me. That's why he's acting so nice.

The world we live in is often an ice-cold one. People are looking for warmth. Just think how good it makes you feel when you meet a really nice, friendly girl ... someone who tells you you're handsome or witty or a great dresser. It makes you want to be with that girl, spend time with her. You get the feeling she understands and appreciates you.

Women work the same way. They want you to be nice to them. Because it makes them feel good. And when you make them feel good, they reward you. With dates. And sex. And love.

If you're a genuinely nice guy, or at least know how to act nice, then you'll be good at picking up girls. Remember, when it comes to picking up women, nice guys finish first.

BE GALLANT

If you're not a creep, and you don't hurt anybody, you're already a step ahead. But if you take being nice to the extreme you might even find yourself a giant leap ahead of other guys when it comes to picking up girls.

One of greatest ways I know to make a girl notice you is to use, what I call, the Gracious and Gallant approach. It's taking niceness to the extreme, and when it's pulled off just right you can have any girl you want — I don't care how beautiful or rich or exotic she is.

I first learned about the Gracious and Gallant approach from a guy named Ernie. We worked in a small advertising office together. Ernie was a smart guy, very polite and quiet — a genuinely nice person. But I assumed his niceness got him nowhere with women, other than in becoming their friend, their platonic confidant. He seemed like the type who spent his weekends fishing with his brother, or holed up in his apartment reading a good spy novel. Well, was I ever wrong.

Turned out Ernie had his eye on Janet, this great looking secretary in our office. (There were five secretaries, but the guys in the office were so shy and stupid we never asked them out). Janet didn't pay much attention to Ernie but he had full intentions of winning her over.

One gloomy, rainy day we were all sitting around working on a new ad campaign when Ernie walks in with five of the prettiest corsages I've ever seen. Quietly, with a soft smile, he went around and handed each of the secretaries a corsage. You should have seen their faces. It was as if Ernie had given each of them a $200 raise and the key to his Rolls-Royce, which he didn't have, of course. All day they were thanking him and telling him how nice he was and how they wished every guy was like him. By the end of the day Ernie had his pick of any of the five girls he wanted, and I don't have to tell you which one he chose. He took Janet out to dinner that night, and a year later, when I left the company, they were still dating. Quiet little Ernie ... I tell you, the man was brilliant.

The Gracious and Gallant approach can be used just about anywhere. Buy a bottle of wine for a girl in a restaurant, rent a limo for your next date (they're not as expensive as you think), offer to buy a fancy dinner for your new female neighbor.

There are a thousand gallant gestures you can perform for a woman, and every one of them will steal her heart. Try being her knight in shining armor — you'll probably find the armor doesn't stay on very long.

THE COMPLIMENT

Most girls spend a lot of time preparing themselves for the eyes of men. Primping, combing, oiling, creaming, and brushing, so they'll be noticed. After all that work, it isn't surprising they like you to tell them how nice they look.

Even if you're not being sincere, a compliment can work wonders. Tell a girl she has the cutest ears you've ever seen and she'll love you for it. Even if in your heart of hearts you know you're only slinging the bull.

I was once standing next to a girl on a very crowded bus. She had an incredible nose. It was about a mile long, but there was something very sexy about it. It gave her a dramatic, gypsy-like look. Getting up all my courage, I looked over at her and said, "Um, I know this may sound a little out of place. But you have a fantastically beautiful nose."

She was shocked. Flabbergasted. "Really?" she said, incredulously. "I think it's terrible. It's so big. I hate it!"

"You're crazy," I said. "It makes you look sort of like a Greek princess. I couldn't take my eyes off you."

The girl was thrilled. I'd made her feel very good about something that had always made her feel very bad. It was the perfect conversation-opener. We very naturally drifted over to other topics. Where did she work? Where did I go to school? What did I do for a living? And so on. I got her phone number and asked her out a few days later. We continued dating for about three or four months.

The moral of this little story is that one of the best ways to compliment a woman is to tell her you love something about her she had no idea was particularly attractive or sexy. Pick out some insignificant little feature she's probably overlooked. Tell her she's got fantastic eyebrows or beautiful slender fingers. Tell her anything as long as it's nice. And don't be afraid to really lay it on thick. Because when it comes to discussing their looks, women are insatiable. They can't get enough!

While picking up girls, flattery will get you everywhere.

SMILE! YOU'RE PICKING UP A GIRL

Most men have no idea what an incredibly powerful turn-on a smile can be. Not dumb hillbilly smiles. And not phony Hollywood smiles flashing acres and acres of capped white teeth.

I'm talking about a pleasant, sincere, warm, honest smile. To women, it's dynamite. Almost every member of The Fabulous Twenty-Five said a guy looks handsomer when he's smiling. The girls spoke of certain men having "cute smiles" or "sexy smiles."

When you approach a woman with an intense, serious expression on your puss, you frighten her. She doesn't know whether you're going to ask directions to the nearest deli or snatch her purse.

Conversely, a good smile automatically melts a woman. Girls want to feel loved and appreciated. And when you smile at them, it makes them feel you love and appreciate them. It makes them feel *secure.*

To many women, a man's smile is almost a sexual thing ... sort of as if you're reaching out to them, caressing them with the expression on your face.

> *Alix:* Most men don't realize it, but a smile can be a very sexy thing. The right kind of smile from a man can actually give me gooseflesh.

> *Marilyn:* When a man smiles at you in a nice, uncorny way, it relaxes you. It makes you like him.

If you have a nice smile, take advantage of it. It's a great thing to be wearing when you approach a girl you've never met before.

What should you do if you don't have a great smile?

Invent one.

WHAT TO SAY

Alright, you see a girl sashaying down the street. She's so pretty, it hurts. You decide that if you can't have her you're going to sign up at the nearest monastery. With great determination, you stride up to her. And now comes the big test. What do you say? What are *the very first words* that will leave your mouth? What's that one magic phrase that will make her tell you, Yes!, instead of, No!

Here are ten great suggestions from our Fabulous Twenty-Five:

Linda: The best thing a guy can do is just walk straight up to me and say, Hello.

Connie: I think a guy should come up to a girl and tell her she's wearing a great outfit or that she has great eyes. He should tell her something positive — that she smells good, that she's the spitting image of Jackie Kennedy, etc.

Carol: Let's say I'm wearing a really wild, sexy hat. A guy should notice that. He should think to himself, now there's something I can comment on. And he should. He should say something like, "That is the wildest hat I've ever seen. You look terrific in it."

Naturally, I'd respond. In fact, I couldn't resist.

Laura: "I saw you and I'd like to talk to you." Or, "I'd like to have a drink with you." Personally, I don't like anything fancier than that.

Mary: If I have a nice dress on and a guy notices it, it makes me feel great. Plus it makes me think, this must be a pretty smart guy. A guy with taste.

Some guys think they have to come on like James Bond, real sarcastic and all. But that's a pain in the neck. It's so damn hard to deal with, to respond to.

I much prefer a man who pays me an honest compliment. But it must be real — not just something he says to every girl he meets.

Monique: I'm not exactly sure what's the **best** thing a guy can say to me. But I do know what's the **worst** thing: "What's a nice girl like you doing in a place like this?"

Alice: Most men think there's some kind of magic word that should be used to pick up a girl. If there is, it's probably something as dumb as, Hello. Just a plain, straight-forward, sincere, Hello, with no wisecracks or super-smooth lines.

Beth: I like a light, humorous, easy-going approach. If a man came up to me and said I had sexy ears he'd have a much easier time picking me up than if he'd said, I want to get to know you.

Marie: Do you have a match? Do you have the time? Aren't you Hank Ryan's cousin? They're all corny, true. But at least they make it easy to answer.

If a guy walks up and says, You're very pretty, what the hell do you answer back? It's almost impossible. You're left there holding the bag.

What I like may not be profound. But it gets a conversation started. And that's what's really important.

Lisa: I like charming men. It really turns me off when some clod comes up to me out of nowhere and says, Hey, you're cute. What's your name and phone number?

I like a guy who .uses finesse who slings the bull a little. The "I-couldn't-help-noticing-you-across-the-room" type of thing is what gets to me. Flowery, theatrical lines — they're fun. They're campy. You can have a good time with them.

As you can see, not all girls like the same approach. What emerges from their answers is that there are three basic approaches: The compliment, which we've already discussed; The direct approach; And the approach that begins with a traditional well-known pick-up line. We're going to analyze the two latter approaches in the next two sections.

DON'T BEAT AROUND
THE BUSH

More women than you'd expect prefer a totally direct, honest approach. No fancy talk. No sweet talk. Just a plain, old "Hello, my name is Joe Schmo." Or, "Excuse me, but you're terrific-looking."

To be honest, this kind of approach terrifies me. One, because it embarrasses me. And two, because I would imagine it would embarrass the girl I was trying to pick up. But apparently I'm wrong. More than one-third of the girls who make up The Fabulous Twenty-Five say the direct approach is the one for them.

> *Bonnie:* The best policy is honesty. If you like a girl, then tell her. What else is there to say?

> *Jane:* I like a very honest approach. It makes me feel a guy is really being sincere if he comes on without any sort of fake charm or wit. It makes me feel he really likes me. And if he can do that, he'll find it much easier to pick me up.

Here's a really inspiring example of the direct approach. It was told to me by a beautiful, young ballet dancer.

> *Monique:* I was going crosstown on the Ninety-sixth Street bus and he (the man who picked her up) got on the bus the same time I did. He was carrying a camera. He sat across the aisle from me and stared at me. The whole

70

time! When I got off the bus, he got off, too. He followed me.

We sort of walked abreast for a half block or so till he finally said, "Hey, look, I'd like to get to know you. You look nice."

It took the breath out of me. I mean I expected him to say *something.* But nothing so direct and complimentary. It was thrilling.

It really was. It was tremendously exciting. Nothing like that ever happened to me before. Anyway, I finally mumbled something about his camera. And we started talking. I gave him my phone number and he called me later in the week. I invited him over for dinner. We had a very nice evening. Not that it turned into any torrid love affair or anything. In fact, I never heard from him again after that. I was sad.

But all in all it was a terrific experience. It was fun. It made me feel good — like I'm attractive. I was very flattered that he'd noticed me like that.

If this kind of an approach sounds good to you, and you think you can handle it, then great. It's the most efficient, direct approach of all. It means that starting a good relationship with a woman can be as simple as saying, "Hi, I like you."

OLD CORNBALL LINES

What about the "Don't I know you from somewhere" kind of lines?

Well, some women like them. And some don't.

My experience has been that, when delivered believably, *convincingly,* they work great. If you say to a girl, honestly and sincerely. "Didn't you go to the University of Delaware?" most of the time she'll think you really mean it. Even if you don't!

If you deliver that same line as if you'd just read it in a book on how to pick up girls, she'll sense you're only trying to pick her up. She won't believe you really think you've seen her somewhere before. And that can often mean the difference between success and failure.

The really great thing about old, cornball lines is that they're easy to handle. No matter what you say, it always gives the girl an oppportunity to say something back. If you ask, "Didn't you go to Ohio State?" she can answer, "Yes," "No," "Maybe," "No, I went to Michigan State," "No, why did *you*?" She and you can spend hours trying to figure out where you know each other from, meanwhile exchanging life histories.

Another good thing about these lines is that they're flattering. People enjoy the idea that you *think* you've seen them somewhere before. It flatters their vanity, makes them feel they have a highly dramatic, memorable face.

A good friend of mine picked up a girl recently by pretending he knew her from somewhere. He first spotted her walking down a city street. She had one of these sensational long, lean bodies with large breasts. He followed her for a few blocks, his heart pounding violently, wondering what the hell to say to her.

Finally, as they both waited at a stoplight, he decided to go with an old, cornball line. "Did you ever work for Thompson Advertising?" he asked.

"No," she smiled. "But I do work in advertising. Maybe we met at another agency."

My friend couldn't believe his ears. Not only was she taking his old, corny line seriously, but she was sort of encouraging him. They chatted for a few more blocks, and then he asked her to join him for a drink. She was delighted.

That night they went back to his apartment. Two weeks later she moved in.

Not bad results from an old, cornball line.

Here's how two of The Fabulous Twenty-Five feel about the "Don't-I-know-you-from-somewhere?" type of line:

> *Gail:* If a man comes up to me and says, "Hi ya, baby, how ya doin'," then I'm completely turned off.
>
> But if he says, "Excuse me, but didn't you go to the University of Chicago," I'd talk to him, even if I thought he might just be saying that in

order to start a conversation.

Susan: I'd prefer somebody to come on to me with something like, "Aren't you Hank Smith's sister?"

That kind of approach is easier to handle — even if I know it's artificial. That way at least I can say, "No, I'm not, but, gee, you must have seen me somewhere else. Where did you go to school?"

75

BE CREATIVE

Another good pick up technique — and possibly the best one of all — is to do nothing but follow your own instincts. Instead of trying to use some line you read in a spy novel or heard on TV, come up with your own. Be creative. Not slick. Don't come on with some ridiculous imitation of what you think the archtypical pick up artist would use. Instead, say something you would *like* to say. Speak from the heart. Say something which honestly, sincerely has popped into your mind.

For example, if you see a girl you'd like to talk to because she's got beautiful, black hair, tell her you'd like to talk to her because she's got beautiful, black hair. If you see someone who's got a smile that makes you feel warm all over, say to her, "You've got a smile that makes me feel warm all over."

A safe, standard line is fine to get something going. But a wild, unsafe approach can be a hundred times more fun and exciting. To both you and the girl.

One night a friend of mine picked up a beautiful French actress walking down the street in Greenwich Village, New York. As she passed by, he said, hello. She ignored him. For some strange reason, this really infuriated him. Suddenly he was overcome by the coldness and the impersonal quality of big city life.

It got him so angry in fact that he ran after the girl who'd just snubbed him and began to berate her. "You know, all I did was say, hello," he said. "But you walk by as if I'm trying to rape you or mug you. What the hell's the matter with you? Why are you being so damn suspicious? Don't you have enough confidence and decency to return a fellow human being's greeting?"

Having gotten this all off his chest, my friend turned to go. He was no longer even dreaming of picking up the girl. He was sure that by now he'd thoroughly alienated her. But just as he was leaving an extraordinary thing happened. The beautiful French actress said, Hello. She was grinning sheepishly. My friend had really reached her. The sincerity and passion and honesty of his approach had broken through her defenses and moved her.

They walked through the streets of New York City that night for hours, talking about everything. Finally, about five in the morning they went back to her apartment and drank a bottle of wine. Then they made love. The big, cold, impersonal city had turned out to be not so impersonal after all.

Try being inventive and creative in your own approaches and you'll be amazed how far it can get you. Again, don't try to invent lines that could fit into a slick Hollywood movie. Instead, be yourself — your exciting, dramatic, inner-most self.

Deep down inside, all of us think of fabulous things we'd like to say to other people. Things that will really blow their minds. Try bringing those fabulous things to the surface. They can really work magic for you.

Here are some wild approaches that were used on The Fabulous Twenty-Five:

Ruth: I was once at a party, it was summertime, and I happened to be wearing a pair of really short shorts. I was sitting on a couch talking to someone and this fellow came over and sat down next to me. But I didn't really notice him.

I was sitting there with my legs crossed, and then I felt something on my knee. I turned and saw this guy writing his phone number on my knee. I cracked up. It seemed to me like just about the wittiest, funniest thing someone could do. We started talking and have been dating ever since.

Lisa: The best pick up technique ever used on me was a really funny one. I was standing in front of my apartment one night with my room-mate. We were just standing there in the door-way, chatting. It occurred to me that we must have looked a little bit like two hookers.

Then a guy passed by and made a remark about us being hookers, kiddingly, of course. I kidded him back, saying, sure, we're hookers. Could we be of any help?

He said, "Sure, what do I get for a quar-ter?" I said, "You've already gotten it."

He laughed. We started talking. He was very nice. I went out with him a few times after that. For free.

Kathy: Last week I was in a shoestore, trying on a pair of shoes, when this guy came up to me and said, "I'm in love with you." "Oh, really," I said, "that's very nice." "It would be nice spending Sunday with you in the park," he said. He said we could have a picnic lunch over a bottle of wine.

Then he said, "You know you look like a city girl." I found this very flattering because I'm from the country and I often feel I don't look terribly sophisticated.

It was really wonderful talking with him. He helped me pick out a pair of shoes. He had excellent taste. Before I knew it I had a date with him.

I felt bad, though, because I had to break it because I'm engaged.

ADVICE FROM THE EXPERTS

Since the first edition of this book was printed a few years ago, a number of guys have approached me with some of their own ways of meeting women. Some of these men were real experts, and some of their ideas were really great, so I thought I'd pass some of them on to you. These are not guys who just picked up one girl one time and that was it. The guys I spoke with were some of the real experts — people I *know* are really good at picking women up, and I was glad to hear some of their ideas. Throughout this book I have been giving the woman's side of being picked up, but you can probably learn as much or more from some guys who have little or no trouble themselves in picking girls up. For obvious reasons, I can't use their real names, but I'll try to give you their ideas in their own words as clearly as I can remember them. These guys are not all athletes or handsome or rich. They are just fairly ordinary guys who have a system that *works* for them. See which of the systems feels comfortable to you and use it if you like.

> *Bob:* I've found that the best opening line for a woman is a compliment about her. The women I meet at the office, in bars, at parties, have spent a lot of time to make themselves look good. And if you notice that, and say so, you automatically look better in their eyes. No matter how attractive or unattractive a girl is there's always something about her that's worth complimenting her on. I usually watch a girl for a minute or two and really study her body and her face. I search for a special characteristic ... one she doesn't expect to be com-

plimented on, like her hands or her neck. Then I just walk over and lay it on her. It always sounds sincere, which is very important, because I've taken the time to find something about her I really do like. Once I've broken the ice it's pretty easy to move into other areas of conversation. The girl feels confident because she already has a hint I'm genuinely attracted to her, and this makes her more comfortable and loose in conversation. If I run into any snags along the way I always fall back to the compliment. It's really dependable, and rarely fails to warm up the chilliest of girls.

Allen: I guess if I had to give this one piece of advice, I'd say "Don't give up if you really want to meet a woman." You don't have to be a pest, but you don't have to give up either. I remember I once saw this really beautiful woman. Both of us were driving our cars, and we had stopped next to each other at a light. I was looking at her, and she must have felt it because she turned and looked back at me. That was the first place I could have chickened out. I could have just looked away or pretended to be staring at something else. That was the easy thing to do, and believe me, I was tempted to do it. But I also knew that I would never meet her that way. So, instead of turning away from her, I smiled and motioned for her to pull over to the side. But she pointed to her watch, as if she was late for something. At the next light, I got out of the car and walked over to her and said, "Hi, I just wanted to talk for a minute, and maybe exchange phone numbers. Why don't

you pull over just to see if we like each other."
So she did. We talked for a minute, and then I
gave her my name and number and she gave
me hers. But when I called her that night, she
seemed to have reservations about getting
together. I knew she was scared, so I told her
I'd call her again because I really wanted to
see her. Well I called her every night for a week
before we actually got together. I didn't push
her, but I let her know very clearly that I was
serious and really did want to see her. And you
know something? We did get together. It took a
couple of weeks, but now we go out regularly.

Mike: The most important thing in meeting
women is eye-contact. Look her right in the
eye while you're talking to her. It's almost like
hypnosis: if you keep on looking at someone,
she can't turn away, and the conversation
keeps on becoming more and more intimate as
you move closer and closer to each other.

Stu: What you have to do when you want to
meet some women is play the situations as
they come up. You have to roll with the situation. When I meet a woman, I don't start by
deciding where the situation is going to lead. I
ask some questions about her and I get interested in who she is, and talk to her about the
things *she's* interested in talking about. I don't
pretend to be interested — I get interested. If
she's into things that I don't know anything
about, I ask questions. I find out the things that
we have in common and we share those
things. I usually find out what kind of movies

she likes or what kind of food she likes to eat.
Those are things you can share together once
you know each others' tastes.

FIFTY GREAT OPENING LINES

Without further ado, here are fifty of my favorite opening lines. Please feel free to use them whenever you want. A lot of guys have already used them with a lot of success. And I'm sure you will, too.

Do you have an aspirin?
(Spoken in a pained voice. The girl will want to know what's wrong. Women love to mother men.)

How long do you cook a leg of lamb?
(You've spotted a pretty young lady in your grocery store.)

Hi.
(Simple but direct and friendly.)

Is my tie straight? I'm going to an important meeting and I want to look just right.
(Use this on the elevator or in the lobby of an office building. Girls love straightening ties.)

I have a fantastic book for you to read.
(You're browsing in a bookshop and you see a pretty girl you'd like to meet.)

I've worked here two weeks now and I've seen a lot of pretty girls. But believe me, next to you, they look like plain Janes.
(Great wherever and whenever you start a new job.)

What color are your eyes? They're beautiful.

(Girls are always very proud of the color of their eyes.)

Where'd you get that great hat?
(To any girl wearing a wild hat.)

Excuse me, I'm from out of town and I was wondering what people do around here at night.
(Use this whether you're from out of town or not.)

I love you.
(To be used half in jest at parties and in singles bars.)

You're Miss Ohio, aren't you. I saw your picture in the paper yesterday.

I'll bet your name is Lisa.
(To you, she looks like a Lisa. Pretty and sexy.)

Are you a ballet dancer?
(Her legs are so fantastic you were sure she was a ballerina.)

Do you have change of a ten?
(You're waiting for a bus, train, etc.)

Is there a post office near here?
(You know damn well there's one two blocks ahead, in the same direction she's walking. Probably she'll lead you there, giving you plenty of time to strike up a good conversation. When she asks you why you don't go into the post office, you confess you only wanted to

meet her. Women find that clever and
flattering.)

Do you like this blouse?
(This line is for department stores. Tell her
you're looking for a birthday present for your
sister and would like her advice.)

Are you French?
(She looks sexy and mysterious is why you
ask.)

Are you Italian?
(She has such fantastic dark eyes is why you
ask.)

Are you Swedish?
(Her great blond hair is why you ask.)

I know you from somewhere.
(You and she can spend hours trying to figure
out where.)

Did you drop this handkerchief?
(Of course, she hasn't! You've just pulled it out
of your pocket.)

What kind of dog is that? He's great-looking.
(To a girl walking her dog.)

Wow! What a beautiful day!
(To be used on a genuinely magnificent spring
or autumn day. In weather like this, everyone's
in a good mood, and the girl you've got your
eye on is more than likely to take you up on
your comment.)

Here, let me carry that for you. I wouldn't want you to strain that lovely body of yours.
(To a girl carrying a heavy suitcase or package.)

Fantastic book! Have you got to the part where the butler murders himself.
(The sexy girl sitting next to you on the bus is reading a book you've just finished. Or even a book you've never heard of.)

You look sad.
(Naturally you don't say this to a girl who looks like she's having the time of her life.)

Come in out of the rain.
(It's pouring. You have an umbrella and she doesn't.)

What do you think of the play?
(It's intermission at the theatre. You see a good-looking woman standing alone in the lounge.)

What time do you get off work?
(To a pretty salesgirl.)

I'm with a company that conducts political polls. Who would you like to see as president in the upcoming election?
(Carry a pad and pencil with you. Look official.)

You look very nice and I'd like to get to know you.

You look sensational in that!

(To a girl trying on a blouse or a skirt in a clothing store.)

Are you a model?
(Any girl will be thrilled to have you mistake her for a model.)

Weren't you Natasha in ＿＿＿＿＿＿＿ ?
(Fill in the name of a play you've just seen. A girl will be incredibly flattered to have you mistake her for an actress.)

You're the second prettiest girl in the world.
(Naturally, she'll want to know who the prettiest is.)

Where did you get that marvellous coat?
(Tell her you work for a clothing company and think her coat is absolutely terrific.)

Please pass the ketchup.
(You're in a luncheonette, she's at the next table, you've got the french fries, and she's got the ketchup.)

If I had a million dollars, I'd buy that for you.
(To a girl admiring a great painting in a museum.)

Didn't I meet you in Istanbul?
(Whether you or she has ever been there is irrelevant. You'll sound like a fantastic world traveller. And she'll be flattered that you think she's one, too.)

Who's your dentist?

(You want to know how she came by such beautiful white teeth.)

Don't ever cut your hair.
(To a girl with long beautiful hair.)

Is there a good restaurant around here?

Would you like a seat?
(You offer your seat to a girl on a crowded bus or subway. Better yet, you offer your seat to her despite the fact there are empty seats all over the place.)

What in the world is that you're drinking?
(To a girl in a singles bar with an unusual-looking drink in her hand.)

Don't tell me a beautiful girl like you doesn't have a date tonight.

If we were in a restaurant, I'd have the waiter send you a drink.
(To the pretty girl sitting across from you in the dentist's waiting room.)

When I see someone like you I thank my lucky stars I'm not married.

Join me outside for a cigarette.
(You're studying in the library and the girl seated across from you is just too beautiful to be believed.)

Now I understand why you have such a fantastic figure!

(To a girl jogging at the track, in the park, etc.)

I'm writing a book on picking up and I'd like to ask you a few questions.
(I found this to be the best picking up line of all!)

MORE GREAT OPENING LINES

Because we all could use an endless supply of opening lines here are some more great ones that have proved eminently successful over the past few years:

Would you like a lift instead of waiting there in the cold? (She's on the streetcorner waiting for the bus; you're in your Corvette — of even your Volkswagen.)

Catch! (You've just thrown a frisbee or a ball her way on the beach or in the park.)

Instead of just sitting there looking bored, how about helping me gather some sea shells! (To Miss All-Alone on the beach.)

Could you keep an eye on my stuff for a second while I take a dip? (On the beach — a prelude to asking her if she'd like to *join* you for a swim.)

Would you mind putting some suntan lotion on my back before I burn to a crisp? (On the beach again, or in the park. It's a bold approach, but makes immediate contact.)

I've been watching you sit here in the sun for the last half hour and thought you might like to use some of my suntan lotion. (The opposite tack from the above, but achieves similar effects.)

Do you believe in love at first sight? (Corny, but say it with a nice smile and she'll eat it right up.)

Ouch! Say, would you mind checking to see if

there's a piece of glass in my foot? (Put that pained look on your face. You're on the beach, about to pass by her when you pretend to step on something. Later on you can claim that it must have been an insect in the sand or grass.)

Did you buy that hat (or coat or dress or bracelet) in the States or in France? (She'll be flattered to think that you think she has French taste and that her clothes look expensive.)

Would you like some help parking that? (She's having trouble getting into a tight spot and you're conveniently there to help her.)

Are you following me? (She's just gotten into the elevator after you and you're both going up.)

Going my way? (Same situation as above.)

You have one of the nicest smiles I've ever seen.

Would you like to go somewhere a bit quieter where we can get a drink and talk for a bit? (The third most common and successful line in dating bars.)

Could you tell me what color tie I should wear with this shirt and jacket? (A great department store line. Follow up by asking if she'll help you pick it out.)

Would you like to dance? (The second most common and successful dating bar line.)

How's the water? (She's just getting out and you've been watching her from the shore, just dipping your toes in.)

They act almost human, don't they? (You're standing in front of the monkey cage at the zoo next to a beautiful redhead. The monkeys are busy nuzzling each other.)

I'll race you to the raft. (Out on the lake.)

I'll race you to the hot-dog stand. (You're out bicycling in the park.)

Can you recommend a really good Coltrane to someone who's just getting into jazz? (She's standing at the jazz counter in the record store and you're asking her for her advice so that she feels like an expert. Obvious variations for rock and classical music shouldn't be hard to come up with if that's where she is standing.)

Say, do you want to see something *really* nice? (You're both browsing through art books at the bookstore and you show her the Van Gogh that you've been looking at.)

Can you tell me who's good for English 438? (You're in the college bookstore at the beginning of the term.)

You can get that a lot cheaper right down the street. (You're in an open-air market either in some big city or in a foreign country, and that luscious brunette is bargaining with one of the merchants.)

What's a girl like you doing in a nice place like this? (At first, they all think it's the same old corny line. But it really stops them when they hear what you've actually said, and if you've said it in a friendly tone, the response is usually friendly.)

I've been studying all afternoon and I sure could use a break! How about you? (You're both in the library, and now she knows that you're really working and not just trying to pick her up.)

Would you like to get a cup of coffee while your clothes are drying? (In the laundromat. Or after you've just saved her from drowning.)

How come I always get in the wrong line? (The line in the bank is moving slowly. But you stood on it anyway just to be next to that pretty girl to whom you can complain.)

You look exactly like Flavia Baccarella! (You can explain that Flavia was your childhood sweetheart and you're sure that they must be related to each other.)

The onion soup is really good. (You're sitting next to her at the lunch counter, and she obviously can't decide what to order.)

Do you know what's good here? (The opposite of the above. She got there first and has already ordered.)

Would you like to smoke a joint? (If she's young and hip, you've got it made.)

Excuse me, do you know of any vacant apartments in this neighborhood? (Whether you're apartment hunting or not this is a great line for meeting girls in the street. Carry a notepad and the classified ad section of a local newspaper.)

Hi, I noticed you, you look nice. My name is _____. (To be used anywhere. Girls are very flattered by this direct approach.)

Isn't that a romantic sunset? (You're walking together, or riding on a bus or just looking out an office window.)

Could you take my picture next to this statue, please?

Could I take your picture next to that statue? It will make the scene look friendlier and more fun to remember. (Either of these lines tells her you're a tourist and invites her to take you under her wing.)

You look a bit lost. Can I help you? (*She's* obviously new in town, and will welcome a guide.)

Can I buy you a drink? (You're both at the bar and alone. The most common and successful line at a bar.)

How do you like the band? (A good opener for a bar with a live band.)

Would you help me celebrate my birthday by having a drink with me? (It doesn't really have to be your birthday. No points taken off for lying just a little.)

I have an extra ticket and would like to invite you to join me. (To someone on line for a movie or the theater. Make sure you get the tickets first, though.)

Could I look at how the stock market did today? (To a woman with a newspaper. Makes you sound like a tycoon.)

You should smile more. I'll bet you look great when

you do. (She looks angry and this may very well get her out of the mood.)

Do you understand what the artist is trying to say here? (In the art museum, in front of something very "modern.")

Do you know if this is worth reading? (In the bookstore.)

Could you recommend a good book for a friend in the hospital? (Again, in the bookstore, but this time you convey the idea that you are a good friend instead of simply someone who's trying to pick her up.)

Do you need some help placing your bet? (At the race track. She looks a bit confused and you, at least, know which window to go to.)

This may sound crazy, but I just bought this lottery ticket and I'd really like you to kiss it for good luck. (Have the ticket in front of you. She'll be tremendously flattered that you think she might be good luck.)

Do you know what the *escargots* are? (You're in a French restaurant, and you ask her to translate for you.)

Look, I'm only going to be here until next Sunday. Do you think you'd be free Saturday night? (You can always change your plans and decide to stay longer.)

What's the difference between primed and unprimed canvas? (You're in an art supply store and she looks experienced.)

Do you work in this building? I'm surprised I didn't

notice you before today. (In the elevator or lobby.)

Would you like to go for a ride on my yacht? (You have a rowboat that you just rented in the park. She's on the shore reading.)

Some friends of mine are giving a party on Saturday. Would you like to come? (To the pretty girl in the neighborhood you've always wanted to approach.)

Are the dance classes here worth taking? (To someone at an adult education center.)

How would you like to go fly a kite? (You have, of course, a kite to fly.)

Can you keep a dog that size in an apartment? (From this point, ask her where her apartment is.)

Does he bite? (Women love to have their dogs petted and admired. They also love to tell you how gentle the dog is, because it is a reflection on them.)

How many ounces in a quart? (In the supermarket. Pretend that you're looking at the directions for cooking something.)

How much steak do I have to buy for three — my parents and me? (Sounds homey — ask her if she'd like to come up for dinner some time: you're a really good cook.)

Are you Natasha, my contact? (Pull your hat low over your eyes and pretend to be a spy.)

What do bean sprouts taste like? (In the health-food

store. Women love to get into long explanations of their fetishes.)

Are you an artist? (She's doing a sketch for her art class in the museum, but you can flatter her work anyway.)

I know you're going to think I'm a male chauvinist pig, but you look like a nice *person,* and I wanted to meet you anyway! (To someone who looks like she might be into Women's Lib. Be sure to emphasize "nice *person."*)

I dare you to go on the roller coaster with me! (At the amusement park. If necessary, double-dare her.)

If you can get away from your parents, I can show you some really nice places around town. (She's in town with her parents, and you're offering her a good alternative.)

Doesn't he have a great sense of color? (You're standing in front of the same picture at the museum?)

How do you like that new Mazda? (She's driving a brand-new car, and you know she'll love talking about it. She might even take you for a test drive.)

How many miles per gallon do you get on that? (She's in a fancy car.)

How many miles per gallon do you get on that? (To a woman on a bicycle, said with a broad smile.)

That dress is great! Did you make it yourself? (Double flattery.)

Look ... I could give you some line, but I just really want to talk without both of us being uptight. So could we skip the formalities? (To be said with sincerity.)

Did you understand what that movie was about at all? I just couldn't follow it. (Either she'll be glad to find a companion who didn't understand the movie either, or she'll be glad at having a chance to explain her interpretation to someone.)

Do you mind if I join you so that I don't have to have my lunch all alone? (She's in the cafeteria and looks bored out of her mind.)

THE MAGIC BOX

Imagine having a "magic box" that could get you *at least* the names and addresses of hundreds of beautiful girls you would just normally pass by on the streets, and very possibly even get you dates with them right there on the spot! Is there such a gadget? You better believe there is! Where can you get one and how much does it cost? Well, if you don't already have one of these magic boxes at home right now, it may set you back about thirty dollars. The gadget I'm talking about is — are you ready for this? — a simple camera! You don't need anything fancy — just any cheap camera will do, and may very well prove to be the best friend you ever had for meeting girls!

The method is so simple that it may make you weep when you think of all the time you've been wasting. All you have to do is ask women to pose for you. Walk around with your little instamatic and take pictures. Take pictures of anything. Take pictures of monuments, of trees and flowers in the park, of buildings, of busy city street corners. But before you take a picture, stand around a bit and wait for some woman who turns you on. When she comes by, ask her to be in the picture. That's all it takes. Say: "Would you mind standing in front of that statue for a second while I take a picture? It will make the statue seem more human." Tell her that you want her picture so that you can remember the scene more vividly. Women love to be photographed. What could be more of a compliment to a woman than telling her that you want *her* picture there to make the scene stand out in your memory over the years? What could flatter her more than the idea that you think *she's* worth taking a picture of? Telling a girl "You oughtta be in pictures" is a "line"; but actully **putting** her in the picture is worth a thousand lines! And you don't even need fancy cameras either. They won't hurt, but even the simplest camera will make getting a shot at a pretty girl a "snap," as they say in the trade.

One further hint, by the way: don't be stingy with your film. Make sure that there is always a roll of film in the camera, and that you really are taking pictures. Usually, just asking your "model" to pose will get you into a conversation with her. But if that fails, for one reason or another, you can certainly get her name and address by offering to send her a copy of the picture. Once you have that, look up her number in the telephone book and give her a call. Tell her that you're the guy who took her picture the other day, and you liked her and wanted to know if she'd like to go out for a drink. Or send her an actual copy of the picture to show her that you're sincere, and **then** call her up and ask her out. Whether you ask her out right on the spot, or call her later in the week or send her the picture and then call, this method is bound to help you meet more women than almost any other method I know.

WHERE TO PICK UP GIRLS

The answer's simple: Anywhere and everywhere. You could pick up a girl on top on Mt. Everest if there happened to be one up there. According to The Fabulous Twenty-Five, if a girl wants to get picked up, she couldn't care less where it happens. Just so long as it happens!

Kathy: I'd get picked up anywhere.

Marilyn: Anywhere.

Lisa: Almost anywhere.

Connie: I'd be willing to be picked up in a bar, a restaurant, at a dance. Anywhere.

This was the unanimous opinion of all twenty-five girls.

Of course, certain places are better for picking up girls than other places. Or at least, they're different. For example, when you pick up a girl in church you have to use a slightly different approach than you would in a local saloon. And picking up a woman on an elevator takes somewhat different timing than on a coast-to-coast plane flight.

So in the next few sections we'll discuss many of the places where you might find yourself wanting to pick up a girl. And we'll try to pinpoint exactly what it is that makes any one particular place different and special from any others.

BARS

In the old days (by that I mean ony about ten to fifteen years ago) it was scandalous for an unescorted girl to walk into a bar. You automatically assumed the worst. And half the time you were probably right.

Not so today. Special singles' bars are popping up all over the country. There's most likely a dozen or so within a few miles of your home. And they're very, very popular. Some of them get so crowded on weekend nights you have to wait for hours to get in.

But, then, waiting is often worth it. Because there are hundreds of unattached girls inside. Unattached girls just itching to find themself a guy. Another added attraction is that most of the girls who get picked up in singles' bars don't waste any time getting into bed with you. In fact I've heard of scores of cases where absolute strangers were making love within an hour after first meeting. And you just can't do much better than that.

So if you happen to be in one of these singles' bars some crowded Friday night, and you see a girl you dig, don't hesitate. Don't knock yourself out thinking up a witty approach. All you have to say is, "Hi, how ya doin'." Half the time the places are so incredibly crowded, the girl couldn't get away from you even if she wanted to.

TRANSPORTATION

If you spend any time at all on buses or planes or trains, you're going to come across some really terrific opportunities to pick up women.

For example, take planes. Sooner or later you're going to wind up sitting next to a good-looking girl on a cross-country plane trip. And if you do, you'd have to be a low-grade moron not to try to pick her up. Ask her where she's headed. Ask her where she's come from. Ask her if you're on the right plane. Just talk. You've got a captive audience. She's going to be strapped into that seat next to you for the next four hours or so. She can't go anywhere but to the bathroom. You've got oodles of time to win her over.

Once you land, help her with her baggage. Share a cab from the airport with her. Take her out to dinner. If you're on expense account, take her out for a fancy dinner. Check into the same hotel she's staying at. Who knows, maybe you'll wind up in the same room.

A good friend of mine almost wound up making love to a girl he met on a train — *on the train itself.* He knew it was going to be a long ride, so he brought a bottle of bourbon along to keep himself company. Lo and behold, sitting across the aisle was a luscious-looking blonde. He started chatting with her. Soon she was sharing his bourbon. And not long after they were necking furiously. My friend was amazed the conductor didn't toss them both off the train.

If you commute to work or school by bus or train,

keep your eyes open for girls you like. Chances are you're going to see them at least two or three mornings a week. Pick one out and try to get a seat near her. After a few mornings you'll sort of automatically become old friends — without even speaking. Before long you should feel quite free to say something to her like, "If this train is late one more time I'm going to personally murder the engineer." Or, "Where do you work?"

You don't need to be brilliant or dazzling. All you have to do is work up the courage to say something. Anything. And in this kind of situation you don't have to be terribly courageous to work up the courage.

RESTAURANTS

In a restaurant your approach can have a special quiet dignity about it. For example, one ancient and corny gambit that can still work like a charm is to use a waiter as your messenger. Have him bring a drink to a pretty girl you spot across the room. Or better yet, instruct him to ask the girl if she would permit the gentleman in the interesting purple tie (that's you) to join her.

You may think it's dumb. But women really fall for this kind of razzle dazzle. They've seen it in the movies. They've read about it in romantic novels. It'll make them think you're suave and cultured and dignified.

Of course, most guys would be afraid to try anything like this. Afraid of looking silly. And that's really stupid. Because the guy who does have the guts to try stuff like this is going to be pretty damn successful. Women like men who are crazy and different and experimental. And not afraid of looking silly. They're more interesting. They're more romantic.

Another good technique you can use in restaurants is this: if you're sitting next to a girl you like (either at a lunch counter or a table) lean over and ask her if she's ever eaten here before. If she says, no, tell her you have and the veal cutlets are great. If she says, yes, tell her you haven't and does she know what's good. This way you've got her coming and going.

MUSEUMS

Museums are fantastic places to pick up on women — especially if you like the serious, intellectual type. When a girl gets picked up while appreciating art, she somehow feels she hasn't *really* been picked up. She's simply met a fellow art lover — who incidentally happens to be a member of the opposite sex.

Wander around a museum some Saturday afternoon and you'll see dozens of single girls appreciating their little hearts out over all the beautiful paintings. You want to know something? Ninety-nine per cent of those girls would give up paintings for the rest of their life if the right guy came by. They're dying to get picked up. That's why they came to the museum in the first place.

I'm not saying they don't enjoy the paintings. I'm sure they do. I just think they'd enjoy the paintings a whole lot more with a little male companionship at their side.

> *Gail:* Museums are great places to get picked up. I love art. And if I meet a man in a museum, I assume he's interested in art, too.

> *Harriet:* A museum is a marvelous place to meet someone. It's so friendly and cozy. It's easy. No one gets uptight in a museum.

The best way to pick up a girl in a museum is to linger in front of a painting until the girl you've had your eye on happens to stop in front of the same painting. Then mumble something profound about the painting, half to yourself, half to the girl. Sort of as if you were so struck by the painting you couldn't keep from expressing your emotion. You'll be amazed at how this turns on art-oriented girls.

> *Jennifer:* You can both be standing watching a painting and then a comment can be dropped. Either by the girl or the guy. Then he can pick you up on your comment or you can pick him up on his.

> In a museum it's not all so obvious. That's what I like about it. It's a very civilized way to get picked up.

A friend of mine was travelling all through Europe's finest museums pulling this exact same bit. He managed to pick up **seventeen** girls in fourteen different museums. They included an especially beautiful Swedish girl, a French girl, an Italian, two Canadians, and a Chinese artists' model, and various and assorted other beauties.

The moral of this story is obvious. Get thyself to a museum and get "struck" by a few paintings. Chances are, a few art-loving girls will get "struck" by you.

WATER

Beaches, swimming pools, lakes — they're all great places for picking up. You'll always see bevies of young beauties tanning their lithe, supple figures at the water's edge.

Don't let them go to waste. They *want* you to approach them. Why do you think they're wearing such incredibly stimulating outfits?

Men often miss the significance of this. It's been said that women really dress for other women. That's simply not true. It's *you* they spend hours in front of the mirror for. It's *you* they're lying around nine-tenths naked on the beach for.

Take advantage. All you've got to do is plop yourself down next to a likely prospect and say something dumb like, Fantastic day, huh. That's all it takes.

> *Ruth:* The beach is terrific. It gives you a feel-ing of, like, you're not really being picked up. It makes a girl feel more respectable.

I don't exactly know what it is about swimming, tennis, golf, and all those other outdoor-type activities. But they all seem to appeal to women as really good things to get picked up over. For some reason sports give picking up a healthy, constructive, All-American quality.

> *Alix:* Skiing is a great place to get picked up. If that's what you want to call it. I call it meeting people. Out on the slopes, standing in line for

the chair lift, sharing a gondola with someone.
Or at lunch in the ski lodge. Everyone sits down
together at those huge wooden tables.

It all has such a healthy, refreshing quality
about it.

I guess you can call it the fresh-air-syndrome.

PARKS

Parks. I love 'em. They are, in my humble opinion, the best place in the world, short of your bedroom, for picking up girls.

What's so great about parks? They have a certain poetry about them. When girls get lonely or depressed they visit parks. Alone. They find a nice quiet place to sit down. And they sit there and wait. For some nice understanding man to come along to tell their problems to.

If you ever see a girl sitting by herself on the grass in a park, you can be one hundred per cent sure she's there to be picked up. Even if she herself doesn't think so. There's something about the trees and the bushes and the gently sloping lawns that open girls up.

A friend of mine is now married to a lovely girl he met several years ago in Central Park in New York City. He first spotted her sitting beneath a tree, reading a book. All he did was walk up to her and say, Hi, what're you reading? That's all it took to get things started.

The next sunny spring afternoon that comes along I strongly recommend you visit your local park. Find a good-looking girl sitting by herself, preferably one who looks a little bit sad. Approach her quietly and say, Pretty day, isn't it. You're almost *guaranteed* to pick her up.

THE TOUCH

Every one of the Fabulous 25 mentioned touch as one of the most sensuous things a man could do when picking them up. A lot of men are afraid to try this, but if you can develop the ability to touch comfortably, you'll instantly make yourself a romantic, sexual figure in the eyes of all the women you meet, and it will go a long way in helping a woman to trust you.

Touching is never done with the ogre-like enthusiasm of a defensive lineman but, rather, gently, sensuously. A man who can touch a woman softly and tenderly without trying to dive down her pants five minutes later, is a man she'll admire. Women will think you're sexy, and you'll notice them looking longlingly into your eyes, leaning softly into your body. All because women love to feel the touch of a man. In fact, every human being loves to be touched tenderly and lovingly by other human beings. It's just something we all remember our mothers and fathers doing, something that we never forget and always love.

That's why touching can be your greatest asset when picking up a woman. It takes nerve, granted, but if you can do it naturally it's a major step to more intimate moments.

Think of the times you were talking to a girl, someone you hardly even knew, when she casually put her hand on your arm to emphasize a point. It sent an almost magical electricity through your body. You instantly felt closer to the girl, like you'd known her for years. Well, girls feel the same way when you touch them. A gentle brushing of her shoulder when you comment on the shininess of her hair, a hand lightly squeezing her knee as you offer admiring words about her shapely body, even a soft caress of her cheek when you tell her how beautiful her eyes are, will melt away hours of coldness in seconds.

Just listen to what one of the Fabulous 25 had to say about touch:

> *Monique:* "I love it when a man naturally, spontaneously puts a hand on my cheek or a finger to my lips. He's telling me he likes my body, that he thinks I'm sexy. That's very flattering to me and automatically makes a man seem sexier.

It seems that too many people, both men and women, are letting one of their most powerful senses, touch, go to waste. Like Monique says, touching can make all the difference in your next pick up.

THE MASSAGE

There are probably three things no woman can resist: Diamonds, flowers and a *good massage.* And when you're trying to become an expert at picking up girls, there's probably no better way to make fast progress than to master the great and sensuous oriental art of massage.

If you've already developed an ease and comfort when touching a girl, and she begins to trust you, you can move on to more elaborate touching and ultimately ... the massage.

Just to give you an idea of how important touching and massaging can be, a major west coast radio station recently surveyed women on their biggest turn-ons. No, intercourse was not the number one answer. Leading the list of turn-ons was kissing or massaging the back of the neck, and close behind, the women said, was having their face held between a man's hands while kissing. The important idea here is that you don't have to take a woman to bed to turn her on. You can do it just about anywhere.

For instance, did you ever see a secretary in your office grimacing with pain while reaching awkwardly behind her to rub her neck or upper back. Secretaries, typists, anyone who sits at a desk all day will develop tension and tightness in the neck and shoulder area. It hurts, and the best thing for the pain is to massage the muscles. So be a hero — walk over and offer to help. It's *very* socially acceptable today and *very* unthreatening to a woman. A little kneading in just the right places (along the ridges of her neck, between the shoulder blades, down the sides of the spinal cord) will work wonders for her pain *and* the beginning of your relationship.

If you find, as many guys do, that massage works miracles for your love life, you'll probably want to get better at it. The best way to learn the finer points of massage is to join a class. Classes are springing up all over the country especially in cities. One of the great advantages of these classes is that they're filled with women ... so you won't have to go far to try out your new skills.

A guy I knew in New Jersey was in a massage class with six girls and one other male. The very first class my friend was paired up with an athletic looking blonde — a gymnastics instructor at the local college. After 20 minutes of massaging her neck and back with almond oil my friend thought he detected a faint moaning coming from her throat. Thinking nothing of it (after all this was just a class), she mentioned wanting to get together for some out-of-class practice, and they exchanged phone numbers. The next day, to his surprise, the attractive blonde called my friend, anxious for another massage.

That night, after just 10 minutes of actual massage, he found himself rollicking around in her big brass bed. He couldn't believe his luck ... and *I* wasted no time signing up for the next class!

If you're in a bar, a disco, or at a party, it might be a little difficult to break out your massage oil and give a girl a full body rub right there on the floor. But there are some subtle ways to show off your talents. Try squeezing the back of a girl's neck gently but firmly while dancing, or run your thumbs inside her shoulder blades and along each side of her spine. Another great and subtle technique is to caress the kneecap — a very stimulating massage for a woman, and not at all threatening.

All these mini-massages are fairly innocent and unthreatening yet they can be tremendously exciting and erotic to a woman. And no girl will doubt your potential for other things if you can turn her on while she's still fully clothed!

So get yourself into a massage class or buy yourself one of the many good books on the subject. It's an investment *she'll* be very grateful you made.

GOLDEN OPPORTUNITIES

Every now and then in life you're going to be thrown together with a woman in such a way that it'd be next to impossible *not* to meet her. These I call "golden opportunities". And they should be taken advantage of with all possible vigor and aggressiveness.

For example, if your seat on a plan just happens to be right next to a stunning beauty, don't sit there like a bump on a log. Talk to her.

If you see a pretty girl at your bus stop morning after morning, talk to her. About the weather. About the bus. About anything. Then ask her out.

Or, if you see the same girl on the elevator in your office building time and time again, say hello. Find out what company she works for. Then call her for lunch.

If you're walking down the street and a girl trips and falls to the pavement nearby, don't race on. Help her up. Then aid her recovery with a drink or a cup of coffee at the nearest restaurant.

Get the picture? It's madness not to take advantage of the "golden opportunities" that throw you and a terrific girl together. They're just too damn easy to take advantage of. And they don't happen all that often to let them go to waste.

ON THE PROWL

No matter how spectacular you are, very few girls are going to try to pick you up. Unfortunately, you're going to have to create most of your opportunities all by yourself.

Which means that if you're really serious about picking up women, you should be working at it twenty-four hours a day. You're going to have to *think* picking up. In short, you're going to have to be on the prowl, ever-alert for even the slightest hint of a possible pick up.

When you step onto a bus or a train, quickly scan your fellow passengers. If there are two empty seats, one next to a fat man and the other next to a slender beauty, for God's sakes, don't be a fool and a coward and plunk yourself down next to fatso. Remember, you're on the prowl. It's up to you to create your own openings.

If you see a good-looking girl in the lobby of a building make sure you get on the same elevator she does. When she gets off, follow her — even if it's not your floor. Pretend you made a mistake. It'll be a good way to make contact with her. You'll laugh at yourself; she'll laugh along with you. And maybe something'll come of it.

A friend of mine once picked up a fantastically cute girl on a bus simply because he took the trouble to sit next to her. There were other vacant seats but he figured why the hell not sit next to someone he really wanted to sit next to. And was he glad he did!

Moments later a huge, horsey woman came lurching down the aisle and stepped smack on the cute girl's toe. She winced. My friend asked if she was okay. She was delighted to get a little sympathy. And to laugh about the whole thing.

A few stops later they got off the bus together and sat down for drinks at a neighborhood pub.

Remember, you're going to have to make your own opportunities. Keep alert to any and all possibilities. You never know when you're going to get suddenly lucky. Simple proximity to women can often result in your picking them up.

MISCELLANEOUS

Here's a few more places that can be great for picking up girls.

Visit a library and sit down at the same table with a dynamite girl.

Take a night course in adult school.

Join your local Democratic or Republican club. Or a more radical or conservative political group if you're so disposed.

March in an anti-nuke demonstration. You're serving a good, sane cause as well as your own personal one. I've heard countless stories of guys who've picked up fantastic women at anti-nuke, anti-draft, anti-anything demonstrations. The point is, if you get involved, you may also get a girl while you're at it.

Try to pick up salesgirls in better department stores. They're often pretty and intelligent. And they get bored hustling goods all day. They're just waiting for some dashing guy like yourself to come along and cheer them up.

Pretend you're shopping for a gift for your mother or sister in a fashionable women's clothing store. These places can be real goldmines because they're simply crawling with thousands of young, good-looking girls.

Go to Church or Synagogue. You'll always find single girls at religious services. And what better way to smooth over the indelicacies of a pick up than to bring it off in a house of worship.

Try to pick up receptionists and executive secretaries. They're sitting ducks because they've got to stay put behind their desks. And they've got to be polite to you.

Go ice skating or roller skating at a big, crowded rink. Go to dances. In the final analysis, go anywhere where there are lots of girls around. This way you'll vastly increase your chances of picking some up.

BORN TALENTED

Whether you know it or not, you already have one great thing going for you when it comes to picking up women. And that is, you're a man.

As a man, it's your right, your privilege to approach a woman anytime you want, while a woman must sit and wait. That may sound sexist in these times of liberation, but the fact is, men and women still abide by and accept this social situation. Women still sit and wait, while men are free to explore all the fantastic female possibilities.

True, women frequently go to singles bars in groups or even alone, and no one thinks of them as loose or desperate. But most of these women still don't feel comfortable approaching a strange man.

Traditionally, a woman without a man is depicted as a tragic figure. But a man without a woman — now that's a different story. There's something romantic about the devil-may-care bachelor who, instead of making constricting dates weeks in advance, prefers to pick up his women wherever he happens to be at the moment.

Consequently, women are a lot more anxious to meet and *keep* a man than a man is to land a woman. And keep in mind that many women have been conditioned to believe that they are losing their physical desirability as they grow older, while a bachelor of thirty-five may just be coming into his own. It's unfortunate, but it's a fact of life. And it's something every man should take advantage of.

Keep this in mind the next time you find yourself shivering with fear at the thought of approaching a strange woman. You are a man. If she turns you down, you can try picking up another woman two seconds later. But she — she may have to wait two weeks for the next man to come along. Or even longer.

To stack the odds even more in your favor, single women in America outnumber single men by *ten million!* In Washington, D.C. women outnumber men four and one-half to one. And in New York there's about three single girls for every guy. That makes you a pretty damn precious commodity if you happen to have been lucky enough to have been born a man.

The Fabulous Twenty-Five said they've found there just aren't enough single men to go around. And these are really *super* girls. If they feel the pinch, you can imagine how tough it is on girls who aren't as talented or good-looking.

> *Mary:* There just aren't enough men in most girl's lives. Most girls I know have one guy to date. Two if they're lucky. But most guys I know seem to be dating eight and nine girls at a time. It isn't fair.

> *Gail:* Most girls these days are very hip to the fact that if they want to meet men then they're going to have to let themselves get picked up. They're going to have to make themselves *available.* The competition for men is murder. That's why girls go out to bars and museums and parks instead of sitting home. They want to be on display and ready for action as much as possible. If they're not, some other girl will get the guy.

GUTS

Here's a fantastic piece of information I learned from The Fabulous Twenty-Five. No matter what a man looks like, what kind of job he has, or what his personality's like, there's one simple thing he can do that will increase his stature in a woman's eyes 100%. And that is, *he can try to pick her up*. That alone says something great about a man. It says he doesn't give a damn for dumb social conventions. It says he's courageous, that he's man enough to go out and try to get what he wants.

Women are really turned on by this. It makes a man look bigger and stronger in their eyes — even if deep down the man is secretly scared out of his wits.

> *Marilyn:* I like men who try to pick up women. It's gutsy. It means they've got ambitions ... that they're not afraid to try new and exciting things.

When you try to pick up a woman it tells her, if nothing else, that you're a guy with enough guts to talk to a stranger, a guy who had the courage to say hello when a thousand other guys didn't. This means a lot to a woman — even if you're scared to death while you're doing it.

Having real guts doesn't mean that you're fearless. It means that you've got the courage to take action even though you're afraid.

> *Laura:* I realize it takes courage for a man who doesn't know me just to walk up on the street and say hello. So I don't mind if he's a little

125

awkward. Or even a lot awkward. The important thing is, he did it. *Despite* the fact it wasn't easy.

That impresses me.

Alix: A man who tries to pick up girls is kind of extra cool. Like, it's an unusual thing to do. It's like a guy adding another twenty-five per cent to his personality and looks. The fact he's got the courage to try picking up girls improves him.

This is all *very* important to know. It should give you confidence. After all, it's nice to know that a lot of girls are going to be very impressed with you right from the start. Just because you had the guts to come up and say hello.

The very fact that you're a guy who approaches girls you've never met before makes you a sexier, more romantic guy.

THE GUYS WHO AREN'T AFRAID TO SUCCEED

A lot of guys who have trouble picking up girls say the same thing — "I'm scared of being rejected". For years I believed these guys, assumed that "fear of rejection" was the biggest obstacle to boy meeting girl.

But recently I've come to realize that most of the time it isn't fear of rejection at all that keeps guys from picking up girls. *It's the fear of success.*

Absurd, you say? Not really. In fact a lot of guys never even try to pick up girls because they're afraid *they will succeed.* And even when they do try, they usually end up sabotaging the pick up early in the game by making some phony excuse why they can't go on ... "I've got to get to sleep early for my 7:45 Calculus class", "I'm just not in the mood to meet anyone tonight". A girl can sense almost immediately when a man doubts whether he wants to pick her up, and it's a good bet she's not going to stick around to be humiliated ... she's not going to waste her time with someone who doesn't care one way or the other about being with her.

Why are guys scared of success? Well, think about what a pick up means. It means taking the time to talk with a girl, maybe to laugh at her bad jokes or smile when you don't really feel like it. Picking up girls means opening up to her, letting her see a little of the real you, and if you like her, even getting intimate and personal with her. Picking up might mean not being able to comb your hair just the way you like, because there's a girl in your room not three feet away, or having to confess you're not sure how, when *she asks you* to have sex with her. And when the pick up is really successful, when it leads to a deep relationship, there are sacrifices involved. Your life simply has to change ... you might miss the softball game with the guys because you have to visit her parents, you may wind up spending a few extra bucks taking her to a fancy restaurant on her birthday.

The point is, for a lot of guys, picking up girls, talking to them, holding them, making love to them, is a totally new experience. And, as any psychologist will tell you, new experiences are frightening — plain and simple (though guys don't like to admit it, even to themselves). So instead of plunging ahead, instead of going after a girl who's been on his mind for days, months, years, the guy who fears success with women invents excuses for staying away ... "I'm not sure where to take a girl after picking her up", "I'll run out of things to say". These are invented excuses, little artificial problems guys create so they don't have to take action, so they can forever keep their lives safe and secure.

Whether they admit it or not, fear of success is a big problem for a lot of guys. But if you're a guy who can honestly say he's not afraid of minor obstacles, if you're someone who's willing to make a few small sacrifices, if you want to meet beautiful, intelligent, desirable girls more than anything else in the world, then without a doubt you are going to have great success picking up girls. Because *women want men who want them.* They aren't interested in a man who decides half-way through a pick up he'd rather be out drinking beer with the guys. In fact, every one of the Fabulous 25 said she'd rather be picked up by a nice, homely guy who really wants her, than a Robert Redford type who can't decide what he wants. Nothing impresses a girl more than a guy who's committed and determined to pick her up.

So, throw away the phony excuses. Let your raw, animal passion for women come through. Show her you want her, show her you're not afraid to make her yours, show her that nothing, neither her feigned look of disinterest nor the pack of girls she hangs around with, is going to stop you from having her, and, my friend, you'll have only one delightful problem — too many girls and not enough nights.

JUST LIKE IN THE MOVIES

The Fabulous Twenty-Five were really delighted to get a chance to talk about picking up. It intrigues them. After I got through interviewing them, they asked *me* questions: How come men are so shy? Why on earth don't they approach us more often? Don't they realize how millions of us are literally dying to get picked up?

To these ladies, getting picked up is fantastic. Fun. Exciting. When a complete stranger approaches a girl out of the blue, it makes her feel pretty and feminine and sexy. And *nothing* makes a woman happier than to feel that men find her sexy. Tell a girl point blank that you'd love to go to bed with her. You think you'll get smacked in the face? You're crazy. She'll love it — even if she pretends not to.

For a woman getting picked up is wildly romantic — something that usually happens only in novels and the flicks. It makes her feel deliciously wicked and sexy when she allows herself to get picked up. She *wants* it to happen.

> *Alix:* You should emphasize in your book that men should never be afraid to approach a girl. In my whole life only two men have come up to me. It was great. I wish it would happen more often. It adds a special spice to life.

> *Willie:* It's very flattering when somebody tries to pick you up. I'd be hurt if I were at a party or a bar or something and nobody even bothered to try to pick me up.

This "please pick me up" attitude was something I had no idea existed before I began this project. Probably because I really didn't understand women very well. It never occurred to me how thrilling it could be to a girl to have a strange man approach her.

I found this incredibly inspiring news. It made me realize that a woman doesn't look upon a man who tries to pick her up as a leering, perverted ogre. Instead she's delighted that a member of the opposite sex not only noticed her, but was so overcome by her beauty that he couldn't resist coming over and talking to her.

Think how you'd react if a girl, any girl, even a plain, homely girl came up to you out of nowhere and started talking to you. You'd be delighted. You'd think to yourself, Wow, I must be dynamite! Women are approaching me on the street. I must be loaded with sex appeal.

Well, women feel exactly the same way when you approach them. Remember that. Next time you move in on a girl, think to yourself, I'm doing her a *favor.* I'm about to bring a little excitement and drama and romance into her life.

> *Carol:* I *like* to be approached. I feel complimented by it. It makes me feel I'm attractive. There's a certain excitement in being approached by a stranger. Maybe it's because you don't know anything about each other. It's mysterious and sexy, just like in the movies.

SADIE HAWKINS COMPLEX

The more I talked to the Fabulous Twenty-Five, the more I noticed a fascinating phenomenon: They want to do the picking up themselves. They're impatient with men. It's killing them that so many guys are so shy and cautious.

> *Gail:* To me it's terribly frustrating that it's not the woman's role to pick up men. Sometimes, if I'm captivated by somebody *I'll* say something to him.
>
> I can't understand why men are such chickens. I mean here we girls are just dying to get picked up. And most guys are afraid we'll reject them. It's crazy when you really think about it.
>
> *Angela:* You're on a bus and a guy offers you a seat. If he looks interesting, you *try* to get yourself picked up. You ask him where something is, even if you already know where you're going. For instance, you pretend you want to know where a certain antique shop is; you pick someplace interesting, someplace that sets you apart as an interesting person. Then, if he's interested in antiques, you've got a conversation going.

One girl, tall, extremely attractive, and with a master's degree in history, expressed the intense frustration she feels that men and women who *should* get together *don't* get together.

133

Helen: I wish men would have more nerve when it comes to picking up girls. Many times I've seen men who I knew were attracted to me. There was no reason in the world why they couldn't have come over and started a conversation. But they didn't. Because they were shy. Because they thought I would rebuff them. It's really sad when you think about it. I mean here I am, dying to meet them. Their intuition should tell them that. Whenever something like that happens it takes all my self-control to keep me from going over and approaching the man myself.

HOW TO GET WOMEN
TO PICK YOU UP

This is a tough one.

Even with Women's Lib and ERA coming into its own, it's going to be a long time before the average girl can approach a strange man without feeling a little loose and a little desperate.

There is, however, one simple but *brilliant* technique you can use to get women to pick you up. And that is, *hang around in places where there are scores of women and almost no men.*

For example, join a ballet class. I know, what would a big, tough, masculine guy like you do in a *ballet class*? Get picked up, that's what!

There are hundreds of places in this country that give ballet lessons. Courses are open to both women *and* men. Take advantage of this. If you've got the guts to sign up, I *guarantee* you incredible success! First, because nine times out of ten you'll be the only guy in class. And, second, because women are almost unbelievably competitive. They'll fight like cats to win your attention. And *affection.* If she met you at a party any one or even all of these girls might have found you totally dull. But in an environment where you're the only guy around, each and every one of them will show great interest in you.

Naturally, if you do take a ballet class you may worry your classmates will think you're gay. Don't worry.

You're a real man and your natural masculinity will shine through. Loud and clear. And all those luscious ladies in your class will compete for your attention.

Where else can you find loads of women and almost no men? In many art and cooking courses. Sure, it's strange and different to see a man among all those women. But your rich, luxurious love life will more than make up for any initial discomfort you feel.

Another great place where you'll run into hundreds of women and very few men is on the campus of an all-girls college. Pretend you've got an important research project you're working on and spend a few hours in the library of a woman's college. More girls will try to pick you up in twenty minutes than in an ordinary lifetime.

How do you get girls to pick you up? By arranging it so you're the only man around.

MORE UNEXPECTED PLACES TO MEET WOMEN

If you just feel too foolish joining a ballet or cooking class there is still one place you shouldn't miss — yoga class. Classes are almost always coed and there's generally only a few male students, so competition is slim.

What you usually find at a yoga class is a room full of skimpily-clad women, with tremendously supple, lithe bodies, twisting themselves into the most delightful and revealing of positions. A yoga class is truly a girl-lovers paradise.

There are also some added benefits to these classes. Most are equipped with a *sauna* ... but just one, and it's always coed. I must say I was a little taken back the first time I went to a class in New York City, and finished up in the sauna talking casually to three gorgeous, completely naked women. You'd think something so sinfully much fun would be illegal, but it's not!

Yoga classes are also cheap, never being more than 5 or 6 dollars for an hour session, and they're easy to find. Schools exist nearly everywhere and more are springing up daily. Plus, if you attend a class regularly you'll begin to look and feel great, a benefit which can only help your chances of meeting a fantastic female classmate.

Another unexpected place to meet women that few men think of is a beauty salon. Don't laugh, I had a friend, Carl, who sold college textbooks. He was always traveling, and he had a pretty lonely life until he discovered the magic of the beauty salon. He'd leaf through the yellow pages, upon arriving in a city, until he found a salon located in the most crowded part of town. Then he'd call for an appointment. There's no law that says beauty salons can't cut men's hair, and with competition between these places what it is today, they'll gladly accept anyone with hair.

Once at the salon, Carl would talk to any one of many women hanging around getting their hair done, their legs waxed, or their fingernails manicured. He explained his presence by saying that he got a much better haircut here than in a regular men's barber shop. He always managed to find a date for dinner, and usually a companion for his entire visit. Carl probably had the shortest hair of any guy I knew, but he also had a woman in every city on the map.

You can also try these unexpected places for good pick-up possibilities:

Art/painting classes, dance classes, massage classes, unisex clothing boutiques, health food stores, pet stores (Hang around by the cute, little puppies), hospital restaurants (I know it sounds weird but these restaurants serve anyone, and there's no better place to meet the nursing staff), bookstores (you won't believe the number of women browsing around), and movie matinees (you'll find a multitude of lonely, mostly married women at the Wednesday matinee).

Just use a little imagination and you'll find a host of places to meet women ... places where women don't expect to get picked up, and where you have the best chance of succeeding.

TAKE YOUR TIME

Maybe you think that picking up a woman means getting her into bed with you minutes after meeting her. Otherwise you're a failure.

And maybe that's discouraged you because you think speedy action like that is next to impossible. You feel destined to be a failure.

Let's get one thing straight. Picking up a woman does *not* mean getting her into bed with you minutes after meeting her. What it *does* mean is simply this: Meeting a woman without being formally introduced to her by a third party.

If you do happen to sleep with her right away, terrific. But if you do nothing but get her phone number you've still been plenty successful. *You have still picked her up.*

If the whole idea of meeting a strange girl and bringing things instantly to a bed seems like a frightening, impossible chore, then take your time. Start out by collecting a few phone numbers. After all, there's still lots of girls around who don't want to be hustled into bed before they even know your name ... who prefer you to take them out a few times before you take off their clothes.

Also, just getting phone numbers can be pretty hot stuff. For example, you could meet a girl Friday at noon and get her phone number. You could call her that afternoon and make a date for that night. And then you could take her out and go to bed with her that night. Which wouldn't exactly tax your patience, would it?

THE ONE MONTH
PRACTICE PLAN

Picking up girls for the first time is like facing a freezing ocean in which you plan to go swimming. Some guys like to hurl themselves in bodily. Others prefer easing in, a step at a time.

If you're the easing in type, maybe you should try The One Month Practice Plan. It works like this.

Allot yourself one month. During this time *try* to pick up girls. But only for the practice. Expect to get rejected. It's only natural. You're a newcomer to the trade and you're only practicing.

While you're practicing, learn as much as you can. Develop a feel for picking up. But never forget that you're only practicing. This way, if you do get rejected, you won't have to take it personally. The pressure to succeed won't be so great. And the disappointment of failure will be negligible. After all, you're only practicing. You can be more relaxed and open about the whole thing.

Of course, don't be surprised if some pretty girl doesn't realize you're only practicing and enthusiastically takes you up on your approach. But then that won't be so hard to take, will it?

BE COOL

A large part of picking up girls is hanging on to them once you've made intitial contact. Just because you've been successful at flagging some woman's attention doesn't mean she's going to come with you right then and there, or accept a date, or even give you her phone number.

So how do you keep them enthralled once you've overcome the problem of getting them to notice you in the first place? The first thing is to keep your head. Be cool. Don't go all to pieces. Don't worry, How am I doing? Does she like me? Does she love me? Will she think I'm ugly? Did I say something wrong? Is my breath bad? Will she notice the pimple on my chin?

STOP WORRYING. While you're standing there talking to her, the girl is probably wondering the exact same thing. Do you think she's flat-chested? Did you notice the scar on her thumb? Etc.

It's the people who act most nonchalant and least uptight, most unafraid of failure, who do the best. If you can get yourself to relax and tell yourself you're doing fine, you'll improve your pick up success ten thousand per cent. I haven't quite figured out the dynamics of it. But I do know that people who can keep from panicking do a lot better than people who become nervous wrecks.

> *Helen:* After the first sentence, things work themselves out. Automatically. They always do.

HER NAME IS MUSIC
TO HER EARS

Here's a great little technique to use once you've made contact. As soon as you can, find out the girl's name. Then, as soon as you do, use it. Plenty. Carol and Jane and Claire and Bernice her to death. She'll love it.

How come? Because the most rewarding moment in a man-woman relationship is when the other person first says your name. It's a sign of affection. Think about it. Think how nice it is when a girl you're just getting to know calls you Bob or Bill or Harry. Or whatever your name happens to be. It's nice. It's tender. It makes you feel she likes you. It makes you feel your relationship with her is progressing, that she's beginning to like you.

Women feel the same way you do. Their name is literally music to their ears. When you say a woman's name with warmth and feeling, it makes her feel warm. It flatters her. It makes her like you.

143

WHAT TO TALK ABOUT
AT FIRST

What do you talk about with a complete stranger?

Well, you don't usually begin with a graphic description of your sex life. Or ask about theirs. You don't tell a girl you've just met that your cousin is a drug addict. Or that your aunt is a lesbian. Not yet, anyway. In other words, start off with general, easy-to-handle topics. Nothing too personal. Or controversial.

Unless, of course, she starts it. If, in the first eleven seconds of conversation, she confides to you she never wears underpants anymore, then fine. You can really go to town. And safely assume she's not going to belt you across the face with her pocketbook. But don't *you* start this way. Chances are you'll offend her.

Meeting a new girl is like meeting a new anyone. You don't plunge right in and begin discussing the most sensational or gory details of yours or their sex life. You sort of edge in.When you first meet a new girl, the object is to casually warm her up. Start off with something general, something that won't frighten her or put her on guard. *Then,* as the conversation heats up, try edging her further and further into a corner so that she begins revealing important things about herself. Once you get her to do this, she's made sort of an emotional commitment to you. She'll feel you understand her. She'll feel close to you. And she'll want to feel even closer.

TAP YOUR INNER DIALOGUE

A lot of guys ask me what to say after they've broken the ice with a girl. "Do you come here often" works fine for getting a girl's attention, but it's keeping her attention, and keeping her from walking away, that can get tricky.

One thing you can try is tapping your inner dialogue. What does that mean? Well, have you ever sat next to a girl at a bar, on a bus, at work, talking about the weather, your job, or last year's vacation, when inside your head were thoughts of what a great smile the girl had, or how shiny her hair looked when the sun hit it, or how her perfume smelled wonderful. Try tapping that inner dialogue, the one you're having with yourself.Reach up inside your head and pull out one of those thoughts and say, "You know I couldn't help noticing your eyes — they sparkle like crystal." Or for the girls at work, "You know, work's a drag but you've got such a great personality you cheer me up everytime I see you." Or how about on the bus commuting," I was just thinking that if it weren't for your smiling face every morning on this bus, I might just quit my job and stay home."

But maybe what you're thinking about has nothing to do with the girl you're with at all. Mention those things anyway. Tell her about the thorn that's sticking inside your boot. Show her the doodle you just drew on the back of your notepad and ask her to analyze it for you. If you've been thinking about a math test all afternoon ask her if she has any tips on taking big exams.

It's that kind of spontaneous, loose conversation that adds a certain excitement and unpredictability to life. She'll admire your candor and your natural good spirit. When you act relaxed it will make *her* feel more comfortable. And when you're both comfortable, the vibrations are **terrific.**

Just think of television celebrities you've seen on talk shows who say wild, crazy, even outrageous things and have the audience hysterically laughing or mesmerized with interest. Or think of your own friends who are especially popular with girls. You'll probably find that these guys are able to say almost anything around women and the girls love it. These guys have broken the chains of formal conversation, they're uninhibited, spontaneous, even a little zany. They're not afraid to show a girl the heart-shaped birthmark on their thigh, they fearlessly do their impression of a mallard duck in heat, and when the conversation gets dull at a party they're always the first to begin a discussion of the best kissing techniques. In short these guys are a hell of a lot of fun because they're not afraid to kick off their shoes, tear off the straight jackets and say or do whatever damn thing they want to.

So whenever you're with a girl and what you're saying isn't what you're really thinking, if you find yourself painfully groping for words, try tapping your inner dialogue. Chances are she'll love you for your honesty, your sense of fun. And from there it's all smooth sailing.

HER OWN THING

All women have some little thing that turns them on. Stewardesses love talking about all the cities they visit or their dumb, pain-in-the-neck-type passengers. Nurses love to blabber on about fantastic operations and scalpels and remarkable recoveries.

One sensational picking up technique is to find out what the one really big thing is in a woman's life. And then to get her to talk about it.

If she loves Europe, get her to tell you all about her favorite country over there. If it's cooking, ask her what her most exotic recipe is.

When a girl talks to you about her own thing, she somehow feels closer to you. *Sympatico* with you. She assumes you understand the real her. And that can't do anything but help advance your relationship.

HUMOR

Women love to laugh. They love for you to be funny. When a woman cracks up, her whole body shakes. It gets her blood flowing. It makes her think she really knows you, much better even than she probably does. If a girl is tickled by your words, it usually isn't long before she submits to tickling from your hands. Laughter melts a woman. It makes her like you.

So if you're good at getting a chuckle once in a while, don't be afraid to put this talent to work. It can really contribute to your attractiveness. This isn't to say, of course, that you should act the clown. Don't make girls laugh at your own expense. Don't *only* be funny and nothing else. But if you can be witty and amusing, then *be* witty and amusing. Most girls love it.

> *Marilyn:* I've been picked up hundreds of times by guys who approach me in a light, joking way. I like that. It brings a little life, a little gaiety into your day.

> *Harriet:* I may not be interested in a man by looking at him. But if he comes on really funny and witty, if he says something different, something that amuses me, then he stands a better chance than anybody of picking me up.

HANG IN THERE

Most girls are a little bit ashamed when they're getting picked up. They've been taught ever since they could walk that it was naughty to talk to strange men. So women feel a conflict when a strange man, whom they're dying to get to know, approaches them. They know there's nothing really wrong with it. But they can't quite erase all that early neurosis and caution that was drilled into them by overprotective mommies and daddies. And that's why they often act a little colder and less helpful than you'd like them to act.

> *Bonnie:* A lot of girls are hesitant because it doesn't look good to be picked up on the street. Being cold makes it more acceptable in their own little mixed up minds.

> So a man has to persevere a little. A girl will play hard to get but she'll warm up. But that's not me. I don't like that bullshit of playing it cool.

> *Helen:* You learn from childhood that there are lots of things you're not supposed to do because you're a girl. Like sit with your legs spread. Or talk to strange men. That's why men shouldn't give up easily. A woman plays a game, plays hard to get. She doesn't want to be an easy pick up. So sometimes it takes a man a little while.

Unconsciously, when she gets picked up, many a girl feels as if she's doing something wrong. By playing hard to get she feels she's cleansing away her sins.

That's why if a girl is cold and quiet when you first go up to her, you shouldn't be discouraged. Hang in there. Don't be afraid. She'll come around sooner than you think. The only reason she's acting the way she is is because she's afraid if she's too easy and forward and warm right off the bat, you'll think she's cheap or trampy.

> *Willie:* A man should realize that even if a woman seems like she doesn't want to be picked up, even if she's cold and barely says anything at all, he shouldn't be put off. As long as the girls say something, *anything,* then the man can be damn sure she wants to get picked up.

NO TIME LIKE THE PRESENT

There's going to be lots of times in the next few weeks when some super-dynamite girl saunters by. And you're going to think to yourself, "Now there's someone I'd exchange both of my big toes for. I'm going to pick her up."

But then a very strange thing happens. Just as you're getting all ready to approach her, you don't feel like it anymore. You tell yourself, "Now isn't really the time. I need more experience. More practice. Tomorrow I'll pick someone up. I'm just not in the right mood today."

If and when you find yourself telling yourself lies like these I urgently urge you to demand of yourself to cut the crap. When it comes to picking up girls there's no time like the present. Do not delay or you'll find yourself delaying all your life.

Do not procrastinate or you'll see one girl after another waltz right out of your life. Picking up women is not that hard or complicated. With a little spontaneity and courage you'll surprise the hell out of yourself.

Next time you find yourself making excuses not to take action, get angry. Tell yourself this can't go on. Tell yourself, I've got to take action.

And do it. Take action. Right then and there. Say anything. Tell the girl she's got a look in her eyes that makes you weak in the knees. Tell her you love the coat she's wearing. Tell her anything. But make contact. Because once you do, nine-tenths of the battle is done.

Figure it this way. If you try and muff, you'll feel better than if you never tried at all. You'll feel braver. You'll feel at least you gave it your best.

But, then, I'll bet you're not going to do much muffing. After all, you've just read thousands of words about how damn easy it all is. You've just read that almost any kind of approach can work — that is, as long as you make an approach. Put what you've just learned to work. It is good, sound, effective advice. It will help you pick up girls. Hundreds of them.

And that's what you bought this book for in the first place, isn't it?

CAST YOUR FATE
TO THE WIND

Women view it as an absolute tragedy that shyness is keeping hundreds of thousands of eligible men from approaching them.

"Stop worrying," they say. "Throw your fears to the wind. Plunge in and you have no idea how fantastically successful you'll be. Sure, you'll lose a few. You might get hurt a little.

"But for God's sake, don't let that stop you. There's all us millions of girls out here waiting for you — with baited breath. So come and get us. Don't be afraid. In the long run, and most likely in the short run, you'll be successful beyond your wildest dreams."

Janet: If a man gets the urge to pick up a girl, he should just do it. Because if you stop and think about it, naturally all your fears will come to the surface. So just do it! Without thinking.

What have you got to lose? When you try to pick someone up, it's usually a complete stranger. So if she rejects you, so what. You'll never see her again.

Angela: Men should always keep it in their dumb heads that we women are every bit as eager to meet and talk to and sleep with them as they are with us.

Ruth: There must be a million men out there

who don't approach women because they're too shy. *That* is a tragedy.

The girls are right. You've got nothing to lose and everything to gain. So don't dawdle. And don't dilly-dally. Take action. Too many people in today's world want to be one hundred per cent sure they're going to win before they make a move. Otherwise they sit there with their hands folded.

Don't you be like that. Here's your chance to be a bold adventurer and reverse that cowardly trend. Here's your chance to be a real man — gutsy and courageous and not afraid of stubbing your emotional toes.

> *Willie:* I wish to hell men were more daring. I mean, a girl can see a guy on the street she'd love to meet. But *she* can't go over and pick *him* up. We girls have to stand there and wait.

> Girls are looking for romance and sex as much as men are. Maybe more so. There are so many opportunities for men to initiate things. They should be aware of that. And they should damn well do something about it.

Good luck, men. I wish you all the success in the world. And I'm sure you're going to have it.